MW01001580

Lost Souls: FOUND!™

Inspiring Stories About Labrador Retrievers

Kyla Duffy and Lowrey Mumford

Published by Happy Tails Books™, LLC

Happy Tails Books™ (HTB) uses the power of storytelling to effect positive changes in the lives of animals in need. The joy, hope, and (occasional) chaos these stories describe will make you laugh and cry as you go on a journey with these authors who are guardians and/or fosters of adopted dogs. "Reading for Rescue" with HTB not only brings further awareness to rescue efforts and breed characteristics, but each sale also results in a financial contribution to dog rescue efforts.

Lost Souls: Found!™ Inspiring Stories about Labrador Retrievers by Kyla Duffy and Lowrey Mumford

Published by Happy Tails Books™, LLC   www.happytailsbooks.com

The publisher gratefully acknowledges the numerous Labrador Retriever rescue groups and their members who generously granted permission to use their stories and photos.

The following brand names mentioned in this book are registered trademarks and the property of their owners. The author and publishing company make no claims to these logos: Hoover, Home Depot, Lowes, Brillo, Cheerios, Disney, Shredded Wheat, Pyrex, Lupine, Jacuzzi, and Kong.

Photo Credits (All Rights Reserved by Photographers):
Front Cover: Pam Marks, www.pawprincestudios.com
Back Cover Top: Buddy, Emilee Fuss, www.emileefuss.com
Back Cover Bottom left: Pam Marks, www.pawprincestudios.com
Back Cover Middle: Gilly, Nicole Derr, www.NMDphotography.com
Back Cover Right: Keeley, Michael Witt, Bald Eagle Photo Publishing
Inside Title: Buddy, Emilee Fuss, www.emileefuss.com
Acknowledgements Page: Jake, Rita Boyd Photography, Millersburg, OH
P142: Pam Marks, www.pawprincestudios.com

Publishers Cataloging In Publication

Lost Souls: Found!™ Inspiring Stories About Labrador Retrievers/ [Compiled and edited by] Kyla Duffy and Lowrey Mumford.

p. ; cm.

ISBN: 978-0-9824895-4-3

1. Labrador Retriever. 2. Dog rescue. 3. Dogs – Anecdotes. 4. Animal welfare – United States. 5. Human-animal relationships – Anecdotes. I. Duffy, Kyla. II. Mumford, Lowrey. III. Title.

SF426.5   2010
636.7527-dc21   2009911456

Happy Tails Books appreciates all of the contributors and rescue groups whose thought-provoking stories make this book come to life. We'd like to send a special thanks to:

Golden Retriever Freedom Rescue
http://grfr.org/

Labrador Retriever Rescue of Cincinnati
http://www.rescuealab.com/

Lake Erie Labrador Retriever Rescue, Inc.
http://www.lakeerielabrescue.org/

Miami Valley OKI Lab Rescue and Referral
http://www.okilabrescue.org/

Rocky Mountain Lab Rescue
http://www.rockymtnlabrescue.com/

Rudy's Rescue
http://www.rudysrescue.org/

Wild Heir Labrador Rescue
http://www.wildheirlabradorrescue.org/

Want more info about the dogs, authors, and rescues featured in this book? http://happytailsbooks.com

Table of Contents

Bartlett

Introduction:
The Phone Call that Changed My Life

"How did you get involved in rescue?" and "Why Labradors?" are questions often asked by people I encounter. The short answer is "Skooni and Bartlett."

Unexpectedly, I ended up "fostering" a six-year-old, male Black Lab while Marty, of "Marty's Recycled Labs" was on vacation for two weeks. The giant, block-headed dog came to me as Hershey and after much family discussion we changed his name to Skooni (with a twist on the spelling after Skoony Penn, basketball star of OSU where our daughter was enrolled).

Within the two weeks Marty was away, we officially became what we now endearingly call our foster families who adopt their foster dogs, "foster failures." Being an inexperienced rescue newbie, I did not understand the joy in Marty's voice when she heard the news. It turns out Skooni was a dog who would have been hard to place because of his size and age, and Marty knew something else we would come to find out: Skooni would completely change our lives.

I can tell you that, during his life with us, Skooni welcomed more homeless dogs into our home than many shelters see and raised more puppies than some puppy mill (commercial breeding farm) moms. My only regret is that he was not a part of my life for the first six years of his. People wonder about the magic of properly matching our dogs to new families—it is not my magic—it was Skooni, who still helps me to this day, in spirit, matching dogs to their new families.

One October afternoon after we had taken in Skooni, a local area shelter called to tell the Labrador Club where I volunteered that they were about to euthanize a sweet, little, 10-week-old Black Lab-mix puppy with a very crooked, shorter-than-normal front leg. Regardless of the dog's dire situation, the Club declined to take him due to his obvious impairment and the fact he was not a purebred.

Furious, I protested by signing the paperwork myself and putting him in the front seat of my van. Coincidentally, I stopped on my way home to pick up a Lab to housesit, and upon seeing the little pup in the van and hearing his plight, the Lab's owner gave me a check for $1,000 to help the puppy! I was overwhelmed with every emotion known to mankind. I graciously accepted the check and the next day made an appointment to visit an orthopedic specialist. With the couple's permission, we named the puppy "Bartlett" after them and called the donation "The Bartlett Fund." Soon after, Marty retired from helping Labs so, with her blessing, I used the remainder of "The Bartlett Fund" to start what is now known as Labrador Retriever Rescue of Cincinnati (LRRoC).

Rescuing Labradors became a passion for me and for so many wonderful volunteers who help our "Labradorables." That unexpected phone call, and two beautiful Labrador Retrievers, started me on this incredible journey and I've never looked back.

The dogs who find their way to LRRoC and other similar rescues come from so many different situations, the most common being: owners who can no longer care for their dogs due to current economic conditions; soldiers going to war; puppy mills and other back yard breeders; abusive homes. Some arrive healthy and emotionally sound (though unloved); others are broken in body or spirit and need rehabilitation. We simply can't take them all, but we re-home as many as possible.

We know these stories about wonderful Labradors and the people who love them unconditionally will make you laugh and cry. And like these angels, we hope you'll adopt your dogs from rescues and shelters and maybe even feel inspired to get involved with a rescue in your area. It is said that when pets get a second chance at life, they love wholly, knowing this is where they are truly meant to be. Come with us: Turn the page and step into the wonderful world of Labrador Retriever rescue...you, like us, may never go back.

Roncy Roehm, President, LRRoC

Inspiring Stories About Labrador Retrievers

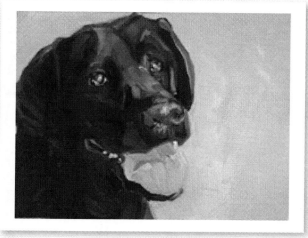

PORTRAIT OF LANCE BY SHEILA WEDEGIS   *savingalabaday.blogspot.com*

This isn't puppyhood: a Good Samaritan takes a battered and broken bait dog (dog used to test another dog's fighting instinct, usually resulting in its death) to his vet seeking help; the vet calls rescue (Heart of Texas Lab Rescue, to be exact); numerous donors pay for surgeries; transport volunteers and fosters nurture said dog back to health; and finally, after so much unnecessary suffering and expense, a loving family takes a chance on this needy dog and finds him to be "the best companion in the world," exactly what he, and his ancestors before him, were born and bred to do. It was a rough start, but Lance finally made it *home.*

When it comes to helping dogs, the heart of humanity shines brightly. Let's keep the torch lit.

The Green Tomato

Imagine that you've decided to expand your household pack to include a companion for your aging Lab. You scour dog rescue websites for a smaller Lab so as to not intimidate your demure girl. Eventually you find a 60-pound Lab who seems perfect, but you forget one thing... *He's only nine months old and still has a lot of growing to do!*

A few months after his listing was posted, our pack takes the eight-hour drive to Wild Heir Lab Rescue in South Carolina, where we are greeted by a growing, 75-poung giant, a dog who leaps couches in one bound!

"Little" Barkley puts his paws on my shoulders and looks me in the eyes. And Maggie, who I at first feared would be terribly displeased with a huge, clumsy brother, is elated. Her infectious enthusiasm hits me, and I can't help but like him, too.

Barkley has no qualms about leaving South Carolina with an unfamiliar pack in a strange SUV. He leaps right in and immediately decides the back seat is simply an exercise hurdle to get to the front. ("Umm, he's in your seat") So I open the door and take him around to the back. By the time I return to my seat, he's back in the front again. Repeat two more times.

Barkley never appears confused or anxious upon arriving in his new home. He paces the bed every night ("Did we get an insomniac?") until I realize he just wants on the bed. His "inch" becomes a "yard," and Maggie and I are now pillows for him to lie on while he buries his nose in my neck. Gently lying down isn't an option—Barkley prefers falling across us from a standing position.

All dogs are friends, all squirrels are foes, and moles are to be carried carefully in one cheek. ("What's in Barkley's mouth?") Leashes and Maggie's collar are edibles ("Why isn't Maggie's collar on? Why are her ID plates on the floor?"); Nylabones and tennis balls are pacifiers; water is for slobbering across the kitchen, requiring a rug to be put down; vacuums are a terror, at times necessitating escape *through* a (closed) Plexiglas door (he wasn't injured); and couches are the place I provide Barkley with a lap to lie across.

Maggie is his most beloved big sister and best friend whose side he won't leave. Her head may be for drooling on, but no matter—Maggie, now 10 years old, is a pup again. Every play session begins with mutual nose licks before pandemonium ensues. Post-breakfast wrestle-mania is marked by joyous sounds of thunder throughout the house and every rug accordioned against a wall. Maggie loves an ambush, hiding under a desk or chair and leaping out at Barkley with a playful "snap-snap" of her ferocious fangs. Maggie lets Barkley chase her just long enough to gain momentum and turn on him - the chased becomes the chaser—and he's as delighted as she.

Beastly Barkley has invigorated my sweet Maggie, and in turn, he has found a teacher and playmate. Like the shiny green tomatoes Maggie taught him to enjoy from our garden each morning, our rescue Lab, Barkley, is young, crisp, and vibrant, leaving us without a dull moment to speak of.

 Edward J. George and Helen Strauss

A Story of Circumstance

L ike so many other stories, mine is one of coincidence and circumstance. Ten years ago I endured major brain surgery and a brief near-death experience. Fortunately it left me with a somewhat altered outlook, giving me a greater sense of compassion for people and creatures struggling to maintain a normal, healthy life. This experience resulted in moments of total exhaustion and despair, but some indescribable motivation kept me going. There were times along the way I wondered why I couldn't stay on the peaceful "other side," but I eventually came to believe the main reason I remain in this world is to not only inspire others with my story but to also find a way to give something back. I just had not discovered what that would be.

Twenty years ago our family moved into a subdivision to be close to schools and other activities for our two daughters, and my wife constantly questioned why we couldn't have a dog. Between my travel and the typical busy schedule of the family, I felt a dog wouldn't receive the attention it deserved. For years I have seen overweight, bored, and neglected dogs that appear to be objects of their owner's amusement with limited concern for the dog's welfare. I explained to my wife that I had no intention of going down that path.

Following my surgery, our circumstances had changed, and I eventually agreed to open our home to a dog. My wife found Sir George, a blind 18-month-old Lab, on the rescue website, and I seriously thought about the challenges he must be facing without the benefit of sight. I reflected on my own struggles and recognized some common ground. Still, we ventured to the rescue headquarters keeping an open mind to all the adoptable dogs. The puppies were especially cute and difficult to resist, but, not surprisingly, they are quickly adopted. As I recall, when the moment came to make a decision, my wife and I looked at each other and asked the same question, "What do you want to do?" Our mutual conclusion was a concern that if we didn't take George, who will adopt him? And so our decision was made. I remember the tears in the rescue director's eyes after hearing our choice. She looked at us for clarification and asked again, "You'll take George?"

Soon after adopting George, my wife entered him in a basic obedience class where he easily became the star pupil. Next we decided on therapy dog training with The Delta Society. Again, he easily passed and has managed to upgrade his status. He visits patients at local hospitals, elementary schools, and nursing homes. The experience is not only rewarding for George, but it also helps those with disabilities and illnesses to connect with a blind dog that is so happy and oblivious of his handicap. During one visit my wife encountered the nurse who retrieved George from an Indiana animal shelter before he was transported to Cincinnati.

Apparently George was severely neglected and his owners were reported to the Humane Society. Sometimes we wish he could tell us his story, but then again, it's probably best if he doesn't remember. We find it far more important that we give him the life he deserves for the present and the future. George and I visit the park often, where he swims and retrieves his ball or stick from the lake. Strangers watch him and are amazed when they discover he is blind. We run errands together to Home Depot or Lowes, and he has become a favorite among the staff. He even tolerates the grandbabies crawling all over him, and we have never experienced even the slightest problem at home. Is it a coincidence that he arrived at the rescue just prior to our visit? I can't answer that, but what I do know is that he is the perfect fit for us.

Often I close my eyes and try to imagine what it's like to live in a world of total darkness. It is frightening for me, but considering that George has no choice, he has learned to adapt by responding to touch and sounds. He groans from delight after a good belly scratch, gobbles his food with absolute gusto, and is excited when he knows we are preparing to travel somewhere. To us he's a big, soft, gentle, loveable teddy bear and a pleasure to hug. I don't know if I would have been so drawn to George and his disability had I not been through a life changing experience myself. Yet the most gratifying feeling for us is knowing George is in the absolute best possible home for the rest of his life, and although he has brought so much joy to our family, it's even greater to be able to give back.

 *Rich Ayers*

Recycled Sam

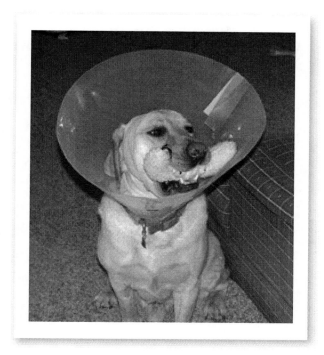

Recycled. *Noun.* To reprocess, salvage, save, reclaim, recover.

December was a busy time for Miami Valley Lab Rescue (MVLR): too many dogs, not enough fosters. I had been looking for a rescue to keep our ten-year-old Lab, Meg, company when I went back to work full-time, so I agreed to temporarily foster to help ease the strain at MVLR and as a trial run of sorts, to see how Meg took to a new dog in her home. My boys liked the looks of a two-year-old Yellow Lab named Sam.

Sam. It was a strong, simple name befitting the big, beautiful dog that ran into my house and promptly lifted his leg on the Christmas tree. Upon hearing my rather startled "Sam!" he made a mad dash to the crate and disappeared. "Well," I thought, "the dog obviously knows how to self-punish." And that didn't bode well in the back of my mind. It was a small taste of things to come.

Sam's history is sketchy at best, but I'm certain family life was totally foreign to him. He had no house manners whatsoever. Not a clue. He could rollover, though. And sit. Petting, or heaven forbid, hugging, resulted in turning and pulling away. Belly and ear rubs were out of the question. Touching his front paws caused severe jerking, all of his leg muscles coming into play as if he were being electrocuted. He had several goofy, quirky habits that we never figured out, such as circling us at a fast pace like a land shark with a toy, shoe, or whatever was handy, in his mouth.

Mealtime was a serious event. Sam would spin like a circus dog, sometimes getting dizzy, staggering to his bowl. While Meg daintily picked one or two morsels, looking around as she chewed, Sam sucked his food down like a Hoover vacuum in under 30 seconds. I know because I timed him once. It's doubtful Sam has ever tasted anything that crossed his palate. He still eats as if there's a canine army behind him just watching and waiting for him to make a false move. Thanks to a four-mile run every day and a long nightly walk, he has the defined waistline we all dream of and weighs in at a muscular 82 pounds. By all rights, he should be as big as a barn.

He surfed counters, ate absolutely *everything,* including a box of Q-tips, two bars of soap, a grill brush (scary), manure based fertilizer (expensive!), a dead mole (no, this was NOT on the counter), and two packages of frozen chicken breasts, cellophane included. My son thought that was cool. "His poopy will come out shrink wrapped," he said. After that I'm pretty sure my neighbors thought I fed these things to Sam in order to make his poop decorative and interesting. The sticks of the cotton swabs sticking out at odd angles were a big hit, but the Brillo-like explosion of the grill brush was really something. How he ever passed it we'll never know.

Leaving the house required advance planning. I called it *Samitizing* and it didn't work. Left alone, Sam was a magician, opening drawers and cabinet/closet doors and dragging all contents onto the carpet. Despite my best efforts, we were on a first name basis with a local emergency carpet cleaning service at $90 a pop. I was so frustrated and angry. I never had these issues with Meg. I could leave a roast on the floor and she wouldn't touch it (certainly not a reflection on my cooking). She didn't eat garbage or dead animals. My mantra became, "Sam's going back. Either that or I will strangle him with my bare hands. I now know why he's been recycled!" Nobody bought it. They knew me too well.

Crating was an option, of course. My brain said, *do it.* My heart said, *not for ten hours a day.*

Sam is a character, a natural clown. His youth was about the joy of living, spontaneity, frequent clumsiness (crashing into a tree while showing off), slowly but surely learning what was expected of him, finding trust, and eating, eating, and more eating. He's sweet-natured without a mean bone in his body (unless you happen to be a squirrel), and I think we were the first to fall in love with him. He couldn't swim, flailing and pawing at the water like a drowning dog. With feet the size of ping-pong paddles he should have pulled through the water like an Olympian. He, to this day, would rather explore and forage for food than swim. A dip on a hot day is fine, but something to eat is infinitely better.

Sam fell in love with Meg from the first. He disgusted her, but eventually she tolerated and finally loved him in return. She was his playmate, mother, girlfriend, grandmother, and best friend. He groomed, teased, wrestled, protected and took all her toys. He became her ears when her hearing failed, her eyes when her sight dimmed. She groomed, frequently scolded, always tattled on, and disciplined him as only an older dog can do. She was the alpha and he was her yellow boy, her fountain of youth, until her death at 15 1/2 years old. They had been together five-and-a-half years.

We often wondered if much was going on in that big, beautiful noggin. Yeah, there is. I found that out after Meg's death when he grieved for weeks, sitting in the front window, watching and waiting for her to come home. He disappeared to his bed for hours rather than being with his family, a big, Labby sigh his only sound. His gentle, brown eyes, the windows to Sam's soul, mourned for his best friend.

I have learned so much from Sam—things I could have done better while raising my children—like stepping away from a situation that caused anger and dealing with it later. I've learned more about unconditional love and patience than I ever wanted to learn. I've learned laughter is far more important than a permanent stain on the carpet or Cheerios everywhere. I've learned that recycling is good and not just cans. I've learned that I love Sam more than I ever could have imagined. He owns my heart and doesn't even know it.

We recently fostered a Yellow Lab named Sadie and then adopted her after two weeks. She's young, sweet, and thinks Sam is her very own plaything. Sam, in turn, is much too patient as she steals his toys. He should flatten her. Sadie is still sometimes nervous and uncertain but getting better with time. She needed us and Sam needed her.

Sam's almost nine now, and slowing down. He sleeps more, his circling is slower and he sits for meals, although he drools and quivers in anticipation. He hasn't run into any trees in a while. He does still carry a toy or my shoe in his mouth when greeting people, no matter who it is. Now I *Sadie-ize* rather than *Samitize*. But things aren't that important anymore.

Recycled Sam, my Sam who wasn't supposed to stay, turned out to be a diamond in the rough. We polished him up and he's priceless. But then, he always was.

 *Linda Kiernan*

Being Found

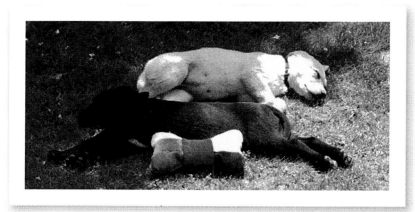

My friend Becky and I had just left Jackson, Wyoming, our home for the past four years. As most ski towns do, Jackson had spit us out, worn-out but full of spirit from numerous adventures. We sought the next chapter in our lives, which called for a bigger town and better career opportunities. But before moving on to a real job and graduate school, we had another road trip and a summer of camping in Santa Cruz planned. With no home, jobs, or places to be, we meandered through the western states, stopping to visit friends in Colorado and national parks in Utah.

While travelling down Nevada's deserted Route 50, we stopped to sleep outside the small town of Ely. It was May and the state campground was still closed for the season, but the gate was open so we set up for the night. After a quick camp stove dinner, a downpour encouraged us to retire to the tent early. The cold, spring rain left us uncomfortable and chilly, and all night we tossed and turned, wishing for our winter sleeping bags. I kept hearing an animal whimper and reasoned it was coyotes in the distance.

When dawn arrived, I was ready to get off the cold ground and start moving around again. We had set up under a juniper tree for protection from the rain, not realizing that it was also an inviting spot for lonely, cold animals. I unzipped the tent door to a yin-yang of fur—one black, one yellow—curled into a ball to keep warm.

"Um, Beck," I said.

"It's just coyotes…" she trailed off still half asleep.

"No, I think they are Labradors."

"What?" she sat straight up.

Just inches from the tent door, two very young puppies had taken refuge under our tree, trying to benefit from our warmth. As we started to move, they woke up and waddled away from us. They were young and scared, but after only a few moments of chasing, Becky caught the black one. I ran round and round the tree without success of snagging the yellow one.

"Here let me try," said Becky, handing me the black one. After a minute or two more, the yellow one gave up and surrendered. In a moment of calm, we paused and appreciated each other: two girls, fluffy (though matted) puppy fur, little teeth, hungry mouths. They sized us up: two girls, gentle and warm, they must have food. Naturally, we instantly named them—Elly, in honor of our strange locale (Ely, Nevada), and Juniper, after the sheltering tree.

Where did they come from? There was no one else around. Did they get lost? They had not been out here long. *And what are we going to do with them?* Becky and I were on the road and planning to live out of the tent for the next three months. We couldn't have puppies.

Then we heard more whimpering. There were two more black ones on the other side of the campground. We put Elly and Juniper in the car for safe keeping and ran after the two others. Boys, we figured, acting tough and stubborn and unwilling to curl next to the tent with their sisters. The closer we got, the more they ran. We coaxed, cooed, and called, but they kept running away. Even onto Route 50. We coerced them back into the campground, but they would not let us catch them.

Frustrated and still convinced that we were not going to keep Elly and Juniper, we left our camp set up and drove into town to find the dog shelter to drop off the girls and report the others. It was still early and the only place open was the diner. "We found some puppies up at the campground. Is there a shelter nearby?" we asked the waitress.

"Puppies, huh? How many?" she asked.

"Well, four. But we only have two right now."

"It's a shame; people are always abandoning puppies up in the woods." Really? Who would do that?

Another customer weighed in. "Yeah, my brother found a bunch up there last week. No one spays or neuters around here, so they just dump them in the woods thinking that they'll survive or something. I'd take them, but I already have six dogs myself. Are they healthy?"

"We think so," I said. "Is there a vet in town so we can get them checked out?"

The customer gave us directions to the vet's office and the waitress provided some sausage for the dogs, both sympathetic to the animals and our situation. We found the vet at the end of town in a small house converted into an animal hospital. Numerous cats and chickens ran around the fenced yard while we waited outside for him to see us.

After a quick inspection, he pronounced the dogs healthy and about eight weeks old. He shared similar stories about abandoned dogs but was unwilling to find them a home. We purchased some dog food and left scratching our heads. Who are these people that dump puppies in the woods?

We drove back to the campsite and packed up our stuff. "Well Elly and Juniper, it looks like you are coming with us." Still talking about finding a shelter for them in California, we began our journey with our new friends. We never did find that shelter, though. Elly lives with me in Boulder, Colorado, and Juniper is with Becky in Concord, New Hampshire. They are nine now and still shy around new people.

The other black dogs? We could never find them again, but we could hear them whining in the woods as we packed our things. Yes, we left them there, but we both knew that they were not our dogs; they did not want to find us or to be found. As we drove out of the closed campground that cold May morning, we passed another truck driving in. It was a pick-up filled to the brim with belongings. We slowly passed each other on the gravel road and exchanged weary traveler nods with the male driver and female passenger. Both in their twenties, it appeared that they had been driving all night and pulled in to get some rest. Those other black dogs found that couple shortly thereafter, I'm sure of it. And that couple now has their own "being found" story, too.

 *Jen Marshall*

Some Gentleman!

It was late August and my task was to bring back selected Labrador Retrievers to our rescue from a local shelter. There among the over-filled kennels he stood, with beautiful, black fur so shiny I could swear I caught my reflection in it. His strong, agile muscles rippled underneath his gorgeous coat, and his eyes were full of intelligence, gold as an autumn field. He watched me soundlessly, but I felt like I could hear him over the deafening barks that sounded like pleas of help. I knew then and there he was coming with me.

"I will call you Gentleman Jack," I said to him as I led him to my car with my other charges. Polite and well mannered, Jack walked right next to me. I smiled to myself, again full of confidence—this one would be easy to find a home for.

By the time we pulled into my driveway an hour later, Jack's behavior had taken a surprising turn and not for the better. I wrote it off to nerves, having seen this sort of behavior in other dogs. Days passed and Gentleman Jack was not improving. In fact, he was only getting worse. Some dogs are needy and learn to cope. But at 10 months old, Jack was needy, entering his teen years, and very smart—a tough combination. Jack had started to figure out how to deal with things that got in the way of his attention from me.

The weather was beginning to turn cold. I dressed my Teacup Terrier, Oliver, in his usual hooded sweatshirt (he chilled easily) and tucked him back into bed. Proceeding to care for my many other charges, I heard Oliver give a quick bark but made the mistake of ignoring it. There were dogs to let out, puppies to feed, ill dogs to medicate, and Oliver would have to wait just a minute more before I attended to his needs.

Then, out of the corner of my eye I saw Jack slide past me...with Oliver hanging out of his mouth! Confused and shocked I ran after him, the rest of the pack also taking part in the chase. I found Jack standing frozen in the yard: tail up, muscles tense, eyes alert, staring at me from thirty feet away. And my little, three-pound therapy dog, Oliver, in Jack's mouth, looking like he was smiling and having fun.

I was a mix of emotions: relief Oliver was okay, anger that Jack had taken him right out his bed, and disbelief that I had just experienced such a bizarre event. What to do... Laughing, sort of, with tears in my eyes, I yelled for Jack to put Oliver down. Then I saw it—Jack was holding Oliver over my Koi stream, where dozens of large Koi were frantically swimming in their direction. I reversed my command.

No," I yelled "Don't you dare put him down!" The Koi were now jumping in Oliver's direction, thinking he was food. Jack was testing my will, not moving while Oliver swung gently above the chomping Koi. As if things couldn't get more stressful, from behind Jack came Sophie, my Doberman, who startled Jack into running towards me. This suddenly became a blessing, though, as I was able to grab Oliver as Jack flew past me. I could have sworn Jack was laughing and smiling the whole time, as is if to say, "I really got you that time didn't I?"

My days continued to play out like that during Jack's stay with me. It seemed whatever I wanted, Jack wanted. He took my food, dirty laundry, clean laundry, and any other item I might want or be using.

Throughout the season, families came and went for Jack. Sometimes they would keep him a month, sometimes only a few hours. Ultimately, he'd come back home to me with the same comment, "Too much energy," every time.

By March I had given up on Gentleman Jack ever finding a forever home and had resigned myself that he would forever be with me. A call came in the second week in March from another couple who wanted to see him. They had seen Jack on Petfinder.com and were smitten. "He is so beautiful," they said (this is how it started with every family). Nevertheless, I again agreed to bring him in for another possible adoption.

The couple arrived at the rescue before Jack that morning, anxiously awaiting him. They didn't even want to look at the other dogs. The volunteers and director had seen this before and crossed their fingers for Jack. Maybe this time it would work out.

Jack's potential new family was a middle-aged couple who were very much in love with each other (they way they tenderly regarded each other made it obvious). They did not have the huge yard we look for when re-homing a dog with Jack's energy, but it was fenced and would work. They had no children living with them, which was a good thing considering how needy Jack was. The man had mentioned he drove a truck route between Cincinnati and Louisville and was looking forward to a riding partner. Hearing this, my heart sank. Jack, calm enough to ride in a truck for hours every day? I doubt it. Jack would be back by Monday, no need to clean out his crate and fill it with another foster.

As tears streaked my face, the beaming couple left with Jack walking proudly and calmly at their side. Jack stopped at the door and looked back at me, his bright, beautiful eyes undoubtedly saying, "Thank you." Then he looked up at his new man and gave a bark. The glass door closed behind them, and the last I saw of Gentleman Jack was his happy face looking up at his new people.

Monday came and went, and Tuesday, too. I started to get notes and emails that they really had expected a more high-energy dog, but Gentleman Jack was just that a Gentleman. Polite and easygoing, Jack spent his days riding in the delivery truck with his new dad. In each letter, note, and email, they thank me for bringing Gentleman Jack home from that shelter and fostering him for so long. I smile and laugh, remembering him standing on the edge of my Koi Stream with little Oliver, dangling from Jack's mouth. Some Gentleman.

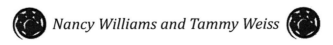 *Nancy Williams and Tammy Weiss*

Life with Labs

The **"Bigg" Presentation:** While camping out at my house for a week, my grandchildren, Hannah and Miles, became so enamored with my foster, Mr. Bigg, they decided to launch a "Mr. Bigg" campaign, hoping to prove themselves worthy pet owners. Their parents returned from vacationing to a vibrant presentation with posters highlighting all of the terrific things Hannah and Miles would do for their dog. Impressed, but unconvinced until they learned firsthand that Mr. Bigg was housebroken, had good manners, and was great with children and other dogs, they finally agreed with the kids. Not only did they then find the perfect home with a fenced yard (they were moving), they also found the perfect dog. *-Carol McMahon*

Discovering Beau

I t all started when I finally talked my wife into at least *considering* the doggie adoption process. Once I had the green light, I quickly began researching available older dogs online. That's when I first became aware of "Daisy's Place," a special program within Wild Heir Lab Rescue that places "mature" Labs and Lab mixes into loving forever homes.

Melissa Gray, Daisy's Place founder, recommended we consider an old guy named Sherman who was somewhere between ten and twelve years old. She told us that a kind lady saved Sherman from a high-kill shelter and contacted the Daisy's Place program. There was only one problem: Sherman was in Georgia and Daisy's Place is in Charleston, SC.

It's a good time to mention that people involved with dog rescue never seem afraid to go the extra mile, and one nice man named Jeff, a member of an air transport charity called Pilots and Paws, volunteered to go quite a few. In his own plane at his own expense, he flew Sherman to the Daisy's Place foster family. It turns out the members of his organization do good deeds like this all the time.

We knew Sherman would fit in nicely with our laid-back lifestyle, so he came for an overnight. His foster mom, Sharon, lovingly packed his bag and dropped him off at Melissa's house for our rendezvous. It was a Friday after work when I went to pick him up. Upon my arrival Melissa introduced herself and then, as if on cue, Sherman rambled in. To some, the sight of a somewhat hobbled, older dog like Sherman could be a little off-putting, but to me he was a very special old soul who needed my love and care.

After exchanging information and a quick good-bye, we helped Sherman into the car. His hind quarters weren't quite as strong as I imagined they had been in his heyday, and he needed a little boost. Of course, once in the car he decided he liked the driver's seat the best. Too old and furry to drive, it took some time, but we coaxed him into the passenger seat where he eventually settled in. On the short ride home, Sherman hung his head out the window and made friends with passersby at every stoplight.

It only took Sherman a quick tour around the house to get familiar with his newest surroundings. Our older male house cat was very apprehensive and watched Sherman carefully as he entered the room. Sherman, however, was much more interested in a long nap in the living room. Just as I expected, he was the perfect doggie guest, going to the door when he needed to go out and greeting everyone like a gentleman.

That weekend, my family and I discovered how much love an old guy like Sherman still had to share. Our fondness for him grew in a short period of time, and we began to wonder about his past. Was Sherman even his real name? We had our doubts—maybe because he didn't respond (we weren't sure about his hearing either, though) and maybe because my wife and I, hailing from long lines of proud southerners, didn't cotton too well to the name Sherman for obvious reasons. Either way we decided that, since he didn't respond to it anyway, we might as well give him a new name. We tossed around a few but finally settled on Beau.

Here's the shocker: When I later discussed "Sherman's" new name with Melissa, she said, "You're not going to believe this, but I'm pretty sure Sherman was a kennel name...and his original name was Beau!" It was clear as day on his medical records; right at the top it said "Beau."

Long story short—checking in with rescue just at the right time, rediscovering his real name, our family's quick affection for him—we were obviously meant to be together. I say this to underscore a feeling I expressed to Melissa shortly after signing the adoption papers. I said, "You know, when we started this process I honestly felt we were adopting him, but after living with him for a few weeks, I now feel like Beau has adopted us." Funny how it all worked out.

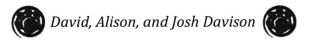 *David, Alison, and Josh Davison*

First Love

It is true you know it when it happens to you. You fall in love at first glance. It is as if you were always supposed to be together.

My mother picked me up at the bus stop early that crisp December day, and I immediately knew something was up. The broad grin that spread across her face confirmed my suspicion.

"I don't want you to become attached," she paused looking at me, "They are not staying."

I shouted with glee. What else could she mean but dogs? I ran into the house, nearly knocking over my dad, and out into our fenced in backyard where two beautiful chocolate dogs stood side by side like mirrored images, inspecting me as I did them.

"They're here to stay?" I asked, knowing the answer but hoping, no praying, I was wrong.

"We'll see," she said, "I am sure there is a heartsick owner somewhere. They have no collars but are well-fed and clean. Very puzzling."

Days passed and I became attached. Of course, any eight-year-old would. Each day I rushed home from school, eager to throw a ball to my new best friends. We had learned in the days since we found them that they were Chocolate Labrador Retrievers; I was in love.

Then the dreaded day came. As I rode to the store with my mother to buy my new buddies a toy, I saw them. One after another, brightly printed "lost dog" flyers were stapled to every telephone pole for what seemed like miles. The picture, obviously of my two Chocolate Labradors, made my heart sink like a brick in my swimming pool.

My mother looked at me sadly; we knew what had to be done. She wrote down the phone number and stuck it in her pocket, and my eyes just filled with tears. It hurt, but love does; my first life lesson learned. We went home and made the call. The owner was so excited and said he'd be right there as soon as he could get a ride. He told my mother he thought they were lost or worse.

I couldn't understand why he waited so long to post the flyers or why he needed a ride to get his beloved doggies. I would have posted flyers and picked up my dogs the first day I lost them! When he arrived, he cried tears of joy at hearing their familiar bark, and the Labs were thrilled to see him, too. He told my parents he had a bit of bad luck lately— losing both his wife and his job - the dogs were all he had left, and when he found them missing, he was devastated. Even though I was a young boy at the time, I could tell they all belonged together and see how much they loved and missed one another.

How did they get out? He explained that his dad had come over to his home to bathe the dogs, and then he had put them in the yard to dry. His dad had no idea the gate latch was broken and so the Labradors' adventure had begun.

Although I hid my tears, I was sure the man could hear them in my voice.

"You will know what to do with this I am sure," he said, as he reached out to find my hand and firmly pressed a plain envelope into my palm. The pain in my chest was like nothing I had ever felt before, so I turned and ran inside.

The next morning at ten we were off to the Lab rescue facility. The fifteen minute ride felt like it would never end. Once there, we were given a short, informative lesson on Labradors, and then volunteers brought out dog after dog. Sadly, I had no matches. They were all great dogs, but none of them felt like my first loves. I was as broken-hearted as an eight-year-old could be. The lady who runs the rescue spoke with my parents while I tried to bond with yet another wonderful Chocolate Labrador named Ruban, but it just didn't feel right.

"I am not sure. We only just got him in Thursday. He's a bit of a wild boy, but if you think..." Soft words were exchanged between the lady and my parents so I wouldn't hear, but I have what my parents call "bartender ears." I hear everything. Seeing my parents look at each other and nod in uniform approval gave me hope that they had one more hiding somewhere...one more chance at love.

This new dog was large with fur so black it was blue. His golden eyes met mine, and he ran towards me as if to say, "I'm here! I have made it!" I buried my face in his thick, black coat and I knew this was *the one*.

"What's his name?" I asked as I ran my fingers through his thick, soft, shiny, black coat.

"Zeppy," the lady who ran the place replied.

"Zeppy?" my mother asked.

The lady hemmed and hawed as if it was a deal breaker, but then she came clean. "It's Zeus."

"What a beautiful name, and Alex loves Greek mythology. How fitting!" my mother exclaimed.

The deal was done, hands were shook. I approached the lady, pulling out my envelope. It was folded and crinkled, but the contents were intact all the same.

"What's this?" she asked smiling.

"It's my reward for rescuing two dogs this week."

"No," the lady said, "It's your reward for rescuing *three* dogs this week!" We all hugged and laughed, and I felt like a grown-up. I had just got my first rescued Labrador and made my first donation to a charity. It had been a really good week after all.

Zeus jumped into the car and sat down right next to me as if saying, "See, I told you so. We were meant to be together."

"Ah, first love," I thought, as I pressed my face deep into Zeus's fur.

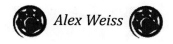 *Alex Weiss*

Third Time's the Charm

Hello my name is Moses, and I would like to tell you a tail-wagging tale about how I adopted my family. For a long time I lived wherever the smells took me, roaming from town to town, just like Tramp from Disney's *Lady and the Tramp*. I loved it! A good puddle for a drink, whatever was left in reach for a snack, and the closest friendly human for a belly scratch.

Then one day everything changed. I met some humans who gave me a belly rub. That was great until they put me in a cage. I tried to explain I had a hot date and supper waiting for me back in the alley, but I wasn't getting through to them and off we went. My next joyride was without the cage - head out the window, ears flapping—what a blast! This only went sour when we arrived at our destination—the vet's office for some shots and a thing called a "neuter." Boy, was that a downer, but soon I was picked up by my foster mom who said she'd find me a permanent family. Maybe she didn't see it yet, but I knew I had already found one.

At home I met my family, including Max and Sam (Black and Yellow Labs, respectively), who quickly filled me in on how great this house is. Then there was Mom, Dad, Grandma, and Sissy. Mom is in charge and taught me the routine. My job quickly became keeping everyone on schedule and in the right place. Dad needs lots of help with this. For example, I often have to remind him that we get a biscuit and a pig's ear when we come inside (don't tell Mom!). Grandma feeds us from the backdoor when we are sunning ourselves in the yard. And while we have to listen to Sissy, she is a pushover for taking us wherever she goes.

Soon I got my first visit from an adoptive family. They were really cool with two kids that wanted to play fetch and hug on me. I went to stay with them for a week, but it didn't last. As nice as they were, I was glad to go home to my *real* family.

Round two at my "foster" home included Sam teaching me how to wrestle instead of fight, and Max showing me to beg from Dad during dinner (Mom and Sissy don't feed us until they're done eating). I then taught Max that all the toys should be lined up side by side in the backyard. Oh, and they're all mine. I liked spending time with Sissy; she seemed to understand my need to hide all my toys and was great for naps and car rides. Out of everyone, *she* would see that I'm home, right? But no, she kept telling me that they were going to find me a good home soon. Stubborn Sissy.

One day I met two brothers who adopted me for their elderly mom. She lived on a big farm, where I liked running and barking at the horses. She reminded me of my grandma, and I knew not to jump on her, but her sons didn't realize that. They got nervous I would knock her over, so she tearfully returned me to the rescue. I tried to reassure her that I was happy to go home, but it seemed like still no one was listening.

Once *home* again, I knew for sure this was where I belonged. I loved them all, and Sissy and I were developing a special bond. I woofed loudest when she came home, and started requesting my biscuit in her room. She began to see my intentions, but only said, "Mom will not agree to another permanent dog in the family." Sissy's other excuse was that she was moving soon and didn't know if she could care for me.

The third adoptive family only sent a guy to represent them, and I quickly convinced him he would be a better match for the other foster dog in our house. He listened, and just like I had planned, Sissy asked Mom if I could be her Christmas present. They talked about it for a couple of days, and I lay on Sissy's lap every chance I got to show Mom how much I loved her.

I only had to bat away three potential families to finally get through to *my* family that they were the one for me. Many years have passed and Sissy and I now live away from the others, but we visit often and life couldn't be better. I love to run with Sissy, whether she's riding horses or four-wheelers, and I still enjoy a walk by myself every now and then (even though Sissy tells me it's not safe). I'm glad I made everyone listen to me about where I belonged, or I might still be on the road, and my family wouldn't be nearly as happy.

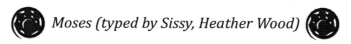 *Moses (typed by Sissy, Heather Wood)*

"**T**he local town drunk brought him in to us, asking if we would help the dog find a home, as he'd found the dog just walking along one of the county roads."

And so Cooper, a young Black Lab, came to foster care with Lake Erie Labrador Retriever Rescue.

Sarah Steiner

The Winding Road...

Molly had come to us as a pup just a year after my husband and I blended our families, and she'd often been lovingly referred to as 'our baby.' Her passing at age 12 gave us several tough months. We all grieved in our own way. My husband missed Molly and said if it were up to him, he'd be done with pets. To this I replied, "I want another dog...just not yet." My youngest came home from school every day with different websites for rescue dogs. She found several, including one "Lab" named Cooper that I said didn't look like a Lab. I wandered through the days, eventually picking up Molly's bed and putting away her bowls. It took months for me to be able to talk about her without crying.

Our decision to rescue a Labrador Retriever was a good one, but the method we used was not. Again, my daughter came home from school insisting she had seen a dog on a website who should be rescued immediately. "It's *an emergency*," she said. I agreed to look. Yes, the dog was pretty. Yes, she looked sad, and with her hefty size she wouldn't be the first on someone's adoption list.

After a few days of thought, we decided to give this one a try. The dog loved us, loved her long walks, and loved the special attention she received. Unfortunately, she didn't like other dogs and attacked two in our neighborhood. Sadly, we gave her back to the rescue organization, a hard decision but the right one.

So there we were, holding out our hearts, only to have them crushed. Weeks passed and my youngest started with the websites again. I was determined to be smart about it this time. Emotion would not carry me away. I contacted a local breeder who happened to be one of the founders of a local rescue group and inquired about a few dogs on their site. I described our recent attempt at dog rescue and stated I was looking for a girl, but when my contact said she'd evaluated a smart, impressive male she thought might fit us, I became interested.

After family discussions and a call to his foster mother, my husband and I decided to meet Cooper, the dog my daughter had shown me *weeks* ago that I'd said didn't look like a Lab! Pictures didn't do him justice—of course Cooper looked like a Lab, but he looked like something else, too. He had long legs, wide foot pads, and a nose like a Pointer. And he was *so* thin! His ribs showed through his shiny coat and there were fly bite marks behind his ears. Cooper met us along with his foster brother but was more interested in playing ball and running around than checking us out. He definitely was a high-energy dog, certainly a change from Molly and her senior citizen days, and according to his foster mom he had some medical issues. Still, we decided to take him.

He came home on a trial that I prayed would become permanent. Cooper's personality emerged and his medical issues improved. He wanted to be near us—to play, run, retrieve—do what two-year-old dogs do. He exhausted me at first; I was used to a twelve-year-old dog. Cooper expected three-mile daily walks regardless of weather and proved to be the best exercise buddy I'd ever had.

We continued to challenge Cooper, practicing his tricks, reinforcing what his foster mother taught him, adding a few more to his routine, and putting him through dog obedience school. It was an adjustment to have a young dog in the house, and not just the energy level! My mother, a wonderful if not continuous cook, was visiting shortly after Cooper's arrival. She'd taken 24 meatballs from the freezer and placed them in a large Pyrex baking dish by the stove. We ran to the store and when we returned, the meatballs were gone, but the Pyrex dish hadn't moved an inch!

Several months later my mother visited again, this time with a baked a ham. Again we had to go out, so I put the ham in the laundry room on top of the dryer. It was in the same Pyrex dish the meatballs had been in. Of course, I forgot to close the laundry room door, so when we returned, we found the ham in the family room with the dish on top of it! How did Cooper get the Pyrex down without breaking the glass? Why were there only a few splatter marks on the walls? Why wasn't the floor covered in grease? Only Cooper knows for sure and he's not telling!

Cooper has been an incredible gift. He's taught us the beauty of second (or third) chances and opening up to love again. He isn't Molly. He's Cooper, and boy, do we love him!

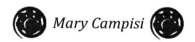 *Mary Campisi*

Life with Labs

A Second Chance: When our Black Lab, Chance, was no longer able to chase balls due to a brain tumor, we had to let him go to doggie heaven. We were dogless for the first time in our married life, until at a stop light my husband and I looked over at the car next to us and saw "Chance!" Unbelievably, the sign on the car said "Adopt A Dog at Second CHANCE Dogs." Within four days we had adopted LuLu on what would have been Chance's 11th birthday. *-Cyndy Woodside*

The Huntress: I adopted Sydney to replace an older dog who passed away. What a surprise! Not only is she a great pet, but she is the best Retriever I've hunted with ever. She points, flushes, and retrieves, and people love to watch her energy. I wish I could clone her. I've purchased and trained two expensive Labs with great pedigrees in the past, but my Lab/Chessie Sydney is the best all-around dog I've had in 58 years. What nice treat for guy who gave an adopted dog a chance. *-Duke Altschuler*

B Quad

I adopted Butch on the spur of the moment. His life-long owner had been in a terrible accident and would never be coming home. He would never see or be able to care for his dog again. For the first two weeks after the accident, the owner's only local relative juggled his own life, that of Butch's hospitalized owner, and Butch's life. The relative worked hard to visit Butch twice a day to feed him and let him out, but it was too much, so a plea went out over the rescue dog email network for help.

None of the local rescue groups, including the one I volunteer with, were able to take a six-year-old, large, male Black Labrador with skin problems and hip dysplasia. I have owned and loved Labs for over 20 years and know it is hard for any to go on living alone in a house with only two visits each day, so I drove out to get him.

Butch's was a love-filled life, but it had some quirks. His owner was a recluse who was afraid to go out in public, so Butch never went for walks. It was just the two of them together, and Butch must have been very sad and confused the day his owner didn't come home. When I met Butch, he had lick granuloma scars, long-term ear infections, recurring skin infections, long split toenails, and a shedding coat in need of brushing. But given Butch's demeanor, his owner had been kind and meant well; he just did not know how to care for his pet.

Despite his previously solitary life, Butch has blossomed. He is friendly to all, enjoys daily romps with our many other Labs, easily accepts new rescue dogs I foster, is fine with our cat, and gets to go to hunting camp with "Daddy Jim," where they have many adventures. One of his favorite activities since the beginning has been deep pond walking. He is tentative to swim, but I think the deep water walking feels good on his hips and has made his muscles stronger.

We can tell Butch's previous owner never disciplined him, probably because he was afraid Butch would not love him. Since coming here, he's been on the training fast-track. At first he put his mouth on me when I trimmed his nails, but he was never very serious about biting me. It took several weeks of trimming every couple of days to get them back to a length so his toes did not splay and he could walk more easily. Now he closes his eyes and enjoys a manicure followed by treats. His skin infections needed many hot compresses, but with a better diet and consistent grooming, his skin has been healthy for 10 months now.

For the first two months he chose to spend most of his time alone in the coat closet. I think it was partly because he was grieving. It took me a couple of weeks to convince him to lie on a dog bed, but now he chooses a comfy one in our bedroom beside us at night and stays with us in the family room during the day. When I brought him home, he did not know much about making eye contact or really relating to people at all. Now he is part of our family, and eye contact on cue has been one of his best lessons. He has very sweet, soft, brown eyes, and I've discovered that he is a sucker for cuddling and kisses (I don't think he got much of that before). Now every morning he asks me for hugs, kisses, nunus, and ear rubs. He continues to develop, and we encourage him each step of the way.

We recently bought a canoe and Butch was instantly intrigued. He sat in it the first day and did not want to get out. Later, he was the first dog to take a trip around the pond. He has the makings of a fine boat dog.

Butch was the name he came with, and we thought he should keep it since he had had a happy life before us, though it hardly fits such a mild-mannered boy. He still does have a naughty side and somewhere along the way earned the nickname "B Quad" (as in B to the 4th) which stands for Big-Black-Bad-Butch. We say it with a smile since he is a softy, and we are happy to have welcomed him into our family where he can live happily ever after.

A year later my rescue Labrador Retriever, Butch, is seven years old and looking better than ever.

 *Amy Reges*

My Chocolate-Covered Yellow Lab

One gray Saturday morning we knew "today was the day" – the one we had been dreading. Our dog, Mandy, lay in the front yard unable to breathe; she had to be put to sleep. I thought, "How unfair of God gave dogs such short life spans!"

Mandy was a Lab-mix I adopted from the pound a lifetime ago. She saw me through marriage (and our honeymoon!), a death, a residential move, job changes, and the birth of three children. My perpetual sidekick, I couldn't imagine replacing her, so leaving the veterinarian's office on that sad day, I said, "I will never get another dog; I cannot go through this again."

But, within two weeks there I was on the internet, looking for our next dog.

We decided to adopt two dogs. My husband, Ken, wanted a male Chocolate Lab and I wanted a female Yellow Lab. I had it in my mind I could replace Mandy, knowing in truth that I never could—we just had too much history together.

With children ages two, five, and seven we had to take care in choosing a rescue dog. I didn't want a male or a Chocolate Lab, stereotyping them as short, fat, and wild. Regardless, on the Miami Valley Labrador Retriever Rescue website I saw a thin, tall Chocolate Lab with a big splash of white on his chest and was attracted to "reformed Jesse's" wonderful biography (courtesy of Phyllis and Paul, his foster parents).

Upon further inquiry, we found Jesse chewed everything in sight. That and his sun-damaged coat made his fosters believe he was left outside. His multi-colored, dull fur was so hopeless that Phyllis and Paul shaved him to make him look better. They surmised Jesse had been neglected but not abused, though the way he jumps at every little noise makes me wonder.

We arranged a visit, and after a four-hour trip we met Jesse playing unleashed in the front yard with Phyllis. At that moment my husband, Ken, knew Jessie had to be ours. The children jumped out of the car and Jesse came right up to us, happily wagging his tail.

Won over, we took him home to Bedford, Ohio, where things quickly took a turn for the worse. Jesse began chewing our children's toys, crayons, and pencils, and took off out the back door after the slightest sound. His foster home had been quiet with two older parents and ours was crazy with three very active children, leaving me to wonder whether this would really work.

When my friend came by to lend us her crate, Jessie seemed to validate my concerns by growling and lunging at her. Mortified and afraid we had made a serious mistake, I called Phyllis and Paul for support.

Offering to meet us halfway in Columbus if we wanted to return him, Phyllis comforted me, "Lisa, I have a grandson the same age as Kenny. I would never have given you a mean dog." There would always be a place in their home for Jesse if we decided to change our minds.

In a last ditch effort we hired a trainer our neighbors liked, who stuck an e-collar on Jesse. Before you get upset, understand we learned from our mistake. Our vet enlightened us to never use an electric collar on a dog, and I got rid of Jesse's immediately. We then tried obedience class but found Jesse simply needed socialization. Our new solution became acquiring that second Yellow Lab I had wanted in the first place.

Unsure if Jesse would accept another dog, we ended up with a Yellow Lab puppy we named "Mazie." She turned out to be the best thing that ever happened to Jesse and has made him significantly braver (except for his continued fear of garbage trucks). There are times when our lives get very busy running around with the kids, so I'm glad the dogs can now be left uncrated in each other's care.

We live by a park where Jesse and Maize enjoy wandering the woods. Jesse will run hard but always stops to make sure he can see me. Each night he comes by my bed for a goodnight pet before crashing with Melissa and Ashley, our daughters (though they often need assistance when he takes up their whole bed). Kenny, who is three, gives him kisses and hugs goodbye each time we leave the house.

The vet says the 20 pounds Jesse has gained this year is mostly muscle, but I think it's a sign of contentment. Though he'll never replace my Mandy, "Jesse Boy" is almost the *Yellow Lab* of my dreams. I know the day will arrive when we have to say goodbye, just as we did with Mandy. I will stand there crying, saying, "I will never get another dog. I cannot go through this again." Nevertheless, a week later I'll surely fall in love, probably with a *male Chocolate Lab,* and we'll begin anew the complicated journey of love, compassion, frustration, joy, challenge, contentment, and then again we'll be left, holding memories that were so much fun to create.

With thanks to our good friends, Phyllis and Paul

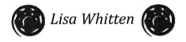 *Lisa Whitten*

Angel in a Dog Suit

This story begins with a cute, young Black Lab being struck by a car and Good Samaritan rescuing her. Said Samaritan then takes injured Lab to a local vet in Sandusky County, Ohio, where she receives temporary care. The vet knows the dog's owners and contacts them, only to find they're "not in..." (...the mood for a dog any longer).

Enter Lab rescue "guardian angel" Suzan Bocciarelli, who takes Molly in. Enamored with her sweet face and calm demeanor, Sue kneels down to greet Molly and is rewarded with a big, slurpy kiss. She can't help but notice, though, that one-year-old Molly does not know her own name. No one has ever taught it to her.

This poor baby is obviously in pain—left hind leg immobile with a major nerve severed when her pelvis was fractured during the accident. Because of disuse, the hock and stifle joints are "frozen" in an extended position and so Molly is left dragging her foot along the ground. Sue constantly bandages the tattered foot and pulled out toenail, trying to prevent further harm. What a mess!

Molly is either standing or lying down; she's too stiff to sit. But despite being injured and limping from car to car as she is passed around between rescuers, Molly is a typical Lab. She trusts that Sue has her best interest at heart and believes her world will be righted soon.

Sue speaks with rescue friends and veterinarians, exhausting every avenue to try and fix Molly's leg. Both her vet and her co-worker's vet come to the same conclusion: the leg probably has to come off.

Ack! It sounds terrible, but both vets also go on to say that "...a three-legged dog is a people magnet."

The endearing youngster comes through surgery with one less leg and a whole lot more friends, proving she's more than just a survivor. Everyone keeps saying, "Oh, the poor princess..." and it sticks. She's a "Princess" now. Funny how she gets the hang of *that* name so quickly...

Barb, a wonderful "dog lady" who until now has had only Newfoundlands, steps into the role of foster and quickly decides that Princess has found her castle. Amidst training, lots of cookies, and love, Princess also discovers her calling—her new mom needs therapy and together they heal each other. Princess regains her dignity and goes on to become a registered therapy dog and a member of Cleveland's Rainbow Babies and Children's Hospital "Pet Pals."

Princess reigns supreme when it comes to sharing unconditional love with others in need. Her magical presence sparked new life into one Amish farmer who had withdrawn to a catatonic state after losing a leg in a farm accident. Though doctors were doubtful about his recovery, after a few minutes of watching Princess stand before him on her three legs wagging her tail, he broke down and gave her a strong hug. From there he progressed to a meaningful recovery.

Amputees and unresponsive patients see this brave dog who swims and retrieves, just like any other Lab, and say, "If that dog can do it, I will try!"

Princess is indeed special, but not in the way you think. It's not her *disability* that makes her special; it's her instinctive *ability* to inspire everyone around her. Now 12 1/2 years old, she is as loving and wonderful as ever. Princess is an angel in a dog suit.

 *Suzan Bocciarelli and Barbara Collins*

Everything Happens for a Reason

Mothers Day was one of the saddest days of our lives. As we prepared to go out to dinner, Shannon, our 10-year-old Chocolate Lab, went to the door to go out as she always did. Except this time she went to the far corner of our yard and lay down beneath a pine tree. Something was very wrong.

We rushed her to the emergency veterinary hospital and were told to leave her for observation—but not to worry—she probably had an infection that could be easily treated with medication. Two hours later we were told to come and say goodbye to our best friend. There was nothing they could do for her. She had bladder cancer and was already in distress. How could this be? Why didn't anyone see this coming? Why Shannon, the *best dog in the world?*

We were devastated, and all cried for days. We still do, sometimes, when we think of her. Friends sent cards and goodies to help ease the pain, and we never thought we would get another dog. How could any dog compare to our Shannon, the dog who listened to us when we were upset, greeted us when we came home, floated in the lounge chair in the pool with us, slept with us, and made everyone want to get a dog after they watched her for us?

Our home felt empty, and after three lonely months we hit the breaking point—we needed another dog. Someone told us about a litter of Black Lab puppies for sale, and after agreeing that we were only going to *look* at them, we returned home with a nine-week-old pup we named "Sedona."

Unlike Shannon, who was a laid back, calm puppy, Sedona was very lively and got into everything. She made us smile again and was starting to finally mature when the unthinkable happened. One day after playing in the yard, Sedona came in with labored, shallow breathing. We took her the vet and, after many tests, were told that she had a heart defect from birth. Making her comfortable over the weekend was difficult because she couldn't breathe when she lay down, and on Monday the Canine Heart Specialist delivered the terrible news. Sedona was in bad shape, and the most humane thing we could do for our nine-month-old puppy was put her down.

We were in shock. Not again. She was just learning to fetch and enjoy quiet time with us. With this new knife in our hearts we vowed: No More Dogs. We could not go through this horrible experience again.

Or could we?

Two days later I received an email regarding two grown Labs needing a home. In the email the owner mentioned contacting a Lab rescue, something I had never even heard of before. Apparently that rescue couldn't guarantee the dogs would find a home *together*, so the owner was seeking others who might be able to take them both. Of course we would have, had they not already been gone by the time I replied. Regardless, the email was like a spark, igniting my fingers to type in an internet search for Lab rescues, which is when I came across Rudy's Rescue in Rochester, New York.

From that point on, each day I checked the website for new adoptable dogs. Although I was told we were not getting another dog, I printed pictures and stories and kept showing them to my family. It took a few weeks, but I finally had them convinced it wouldn't hurt to meet an older dog from the rescue.

The application for Rudy's Rescue was thorough, requiring three personal references, our veterinarian's contact information, and a variety of other personal data. We passed the home inspection with flying colors and after two weeks were finally approved to "inquire" and possibly adopt a dog. The only problem was that by then, all the dogs we were interested in had already found homes!

Believing that everything happens for a reason, we decided to stay on the lookout and see if our perfect old dog would come along. While waiting, I noticed two cute Yellow Lab puppies needing homes on the Rudy's Rescue website.

Fergie's bio made her sound eerily like Shannon—a very calm Yellow Lab puppy. Beside myself, I printed her picture and begged the family to go and see her (it really didn't take much). Everyone fell in love immediately and our plan for an older dog went out the window.

We made an appointment to visit the five-month-old stray at her foster family's house, two hours away. Upon arrival our hopes and dreams turned into reality, and we were greeted with lots of puppy kisses by a beautiful, green-eyed baby. We were the third family to meet her that day and didn't get to spend long. The decision on Fergie's forever family would be made the next day by her foster family. She was perfect—so much like Shannon, so cuddly and docile—we tried not to get our hopes up, but how could we not?

The next afternoon was a nail-biter until the call finally came: Fergie had chosen us. Again we cried, but this time they were tears of joy. We picked her up the next day and she settled in quickly. We've been a happy family ever since. Out of 12 names we came up with we chose to rename Fergie "Bella" for her breathtaking beauty.

Bella's smart, healthy, and even good with the vet. Her sociability and affection have earned her many new friends in our neighborhood, making her a great Ambassador for Rudy's Rescue. She has even carved a niche as "lifeguard" at our pool. Everyone is happy, especially Bella, and our home is again complete. Although our children are older, Bella brings out the "puppy" in all of us—proof that everything happens for a reason.

 *Marylou Ricigliano*

Life with Labs

Best Money Ever Spent: Six-year-old Oona was ahead of me on a walk in the woods, when her ears popped up. I couldn't see what had her attention, so I commanded her to sit. She dropped her rear end where she was standing without hesitation. As I came up behind her, I saw nine deer running through the field, not more than 50 yards ahead of us. Oona never broke the sit, but after the deer had passed, I put her leash on (no sense in tempting fate). As soon as I got home, I called my trainer and told him his lessons were the best money I had ever spent. If we had been with any of my friend's dogs, they would have been long gone after the deer, and we would still be chasing them. *-Tim Coolbaugh*

Howdy, New Mom and Dad! Kia, the unplace-able Chocolate Lab, was not comfortable with the chaos of a young family. It only takes one right family to come along, though. Adopted by an older, quiet, childless couple, she now spends her days sitting on a couch, listening to country music. *-Kimberly Tenai*

The Few, The Proud,
The Customs Service Dogs

Margie is an upbeat, outgoing, athletic Labrador Retriever who would rather retrieve than eat – the perfect disposition for a service dog in many fields. After several months in foster care with Lake Erie Labrador Retriever Rescue (LELRR), a man adopted Margie, planning to train her as a gun dog. What no one knew at the time was that this man really had no prior experience training gun dogs. Of course, Margie ended up back in our foster care, beginning her journey to find a forever home anew.

This time, Margie hit the "dog lottery." In the spring she met Charlie Harris, a trainer with the U. S. Customs Service

Canine Enforcement Training Program. He was looking for dogs with "the right stuff" to become trainees in the Customs program and learn to detect contraband (perhaps drugs, perhaps currency) on persons entering the United States. Margie flew through the various exercises during her initial screening, and Charlie was very excited. So Margie hit the road for Front Royal, VA, where the training center is located.

LELRR has worked with Customs for years, and we are always thrilled if a dog is selected for this training program. Only about 50% complete the course, bailing out along the way because they get bored or find it too challenging. The training is based on desire to retrieve, and the dogs work for the joy of retrieving. Even so, not all dogs are blessed with perfect abilities to scent, and some contraband is almost scentless. Two dogs are assigned to each individual who goes to Front Royal to become a Canine Enforcement Officer; the expectation being that one of the dogs will graduate.

LELRR has always taken the position that if one of our dogs cannot graduate, we will take it back and re-home it ourselves. Customs has a good pet placement program for the dogs who don't graduate, but we feel strongly that we want our dogs back. Thankfully, Customs has always obliged.

Margie and her counterpart both graduated. This was great news, but the very best news was that Margie graduated "top dog" in her class! Margie received her badge at the formal graduation ceremony and went off to have a career as a Customs Officer in the service of her country. We are all very proud of this once-thrown-away homeless dog who has now become an American hero.

 *Sarah N. Steiner*

More than Mischief

I am ashamed to admit that my beautiful girl, Onyx, was the proverbial "free" dog. As she was my first dog, I was woefully unprepared for pet ownership. I did not know about crate training, quality dog food, heartworm prevention, Lupine collars, the expense of spaying, submissive urination, or the Lab penchant for eating anything and everything, including Grandma's rocking chair.

The fact that this dog survived puppyhood is nothing short of miraculous. At first, she was just in poor health with a heart murmur and worms that could be mistaken for garden snakes. Then came the curious/destructive phase:

she chewed through a laptop cord in under five seconds; she went through a screen (teaching me to keep the windows down); she was scalped when she ran under a moving car in the driveway; she learned to open the screen door, even when locked, and let herself out at will; and the puppy who could not step down one single step managed to jump on to the washing machine and drink bleach while I pulled clothes out of the dryer.

Nor did I expect to be standing outside at 3am in a torrential downpour with a puppy who refused to go potty with wet grass tickling her behind. I did not know she would learn to break through the bathroom door (apparently to make sure I did not sneak out the trap door I wish I had in the back of the shower), or that I was committing to 10+ years of showers with a little face peeking at me around the shower curtain or sharing the shower with me each time. My husband and I certainly never expected her to jump between us in the Jacuzzi!

There is more to Onyx than her mischievousness might let on, thought. She had no real say in my decision to become a foster mom with a Labrador Retriever rescue group. Nonetheless, she has greeted 13 dogs in one year, and she has not merely tolerated them, or grudgingly shared her mommy with them, she has been a full and active participant in helping each and every one of our special guests.

When our first foster dog did not know how to come down the stairs (he managed to get up them without a problem), Onyx stood on the stairs with me for the better part of an hour. Over and over again she patiently showed him, one paw at a time, how to come down the stairs. And when I came home with two 10-week-old puppies who were trying to nurse on her, she dutifully mothered them.

When my fourth foster arrived with a raging fever and full-blown kennel cough, neither dog left the couch for two days. Onyx stayed right with her, nursing and grooming, and periodically giving me the "Do something!" look. When I presented Onyx with two bonded senior dogs, she slowed her level of play to include them and even gave up her place in our bed for the seniors to sleep.

Next was a fearful little girl: afraid of her shadow and doorways, who had no idea what toys were or how to be a dog. When she lay on the floor in front of the couch, Onyx lay on the floor, facing her, and started rolling a ball to our guest, slowly and gently. After a week, the scared girl would roll it back, and then they progressed to playing tug-of-war, but Onyx would not stand up; she just remained lying down and patiently showing the scaredy pup how to be a dog.

I don't know why I am continually amazed at her kind and gentle spirit. This is, after all, the same dog who watched the movie "Eight Below" with me. Every time one of the dogs fell ill or died in the movie, Onyx would press her nose to the TV screen and *HOWL* in sadness, mourning right along with the rest of the pack.

Had somebody told me my dog was going to rule my life, dictate a curfew, and sleep under the covers on her back with all four legs straight in the air, thus creating a tent, I would have scoffed at them. Now ask me, having accepted this tiny dictator as my ruler, is it worth it?

Since she has come into my life, I have not cried a single tear that has gone unlicked. I have not been ill one single time that she has not steadfastly lain by my side, grooming me, until I am well again. For her loyalty and devotion and her endless acts of kindness, Onyx asks only that I play Frisbee with her. It's no wonder Labs continue to be the number one dog in America.

 *Shimiah Arner Grow*

The Best Buddy

When my friend's five-year-old son met Buddy, he said, "Mommy, why does Buddy have ow-ies? Can we take him to the vet?"

My husband and I had been fostering three-year-old Buddy. A very regal Yellow Lab, he had the most soulful but sad eyes, which were a window into his tormented soul. Buddy was horribly abused and had telling scars to prove it.

Buddy's back left foot is deformed and a year later, his fur is still growing back in places. When we got him, he was so thin I thought his ribs would poke through his skin. If we raised a hand to pet him, he cringed. Even something as benign as opening the refrigerator sent him into a total panic; he'd bury himself in a corner, shaking in fear. When we would pet him, he'd look up at us with those big, brown eyes, pleading to be loved, telling us he was a good boy but still uneasy.

X-rays showed he had several broken bones in his foot. Untreated, they had fused together as they healed, leaving his foot functional but deformed. He had bare spots on his tail and backside, probably from the same accident which broke his foot (and subsequently our hearts—his emotional and physical scars are so deep and lasting it's sometimes hard to bear).

From day one we knew Buddy was a special guy. He is a big boy but gentle as can be. All he ever wanted was to be loved. To help him heal, we worked with him: feeding him good food to get some weight back on, playing with him, petting him, taking him everywhere with us to socialize him. We asked everyone to stroke him and make a fuss over him, so he would learn that not all people are bad. With his intense "therapy" it didn't take long for him to wag his tail when we petted him. Now all we have to do is call his name, and we receive a loud THUMP, THUMP, THUMP in return.

Buddy immediately bonded with our other two dogs, who would cuddle with him in the evenings as if sensing he needed them. Even the cats approached him, curling up next to him on his dog bed and purring lightly. Now he accepts love with a sigh of contentment.

Buddy quickly learned how comfy our couch was and would lie across our laps, groaning as we rubbed his belly. He'd always thank us with big, slobbery kisses. He loves to sleep in bed with us, and if he hears a car door open, he's right there, wagging his booty with excitement and anticipation of a car ride.

Well, you probably guessed it by now. We fell in love, and instead of just fostering Buddy, we adopted him. I think we both knew from day one that he had already picked us as his family.

Today his past injuries still show on the outside, but his heart is healed. He is our "Bud," and when we lost his Golden sister to cancer recently, he licked my tears away and lay next to me as I grieved. We helped him, but he has returned the love tenfold (as all dogs do).

As I write this, he is sleeping by my side and dreaming... I think he's chasing rabbits!

 *Shereen Raucci*

The Holiday Blessing

The leaves of late fall swirled around our packing boxes, forming little brown and golden drifts. We had just moved into our new home, and I was still lugging boxes from the detached garage into the house. My husband, son, and I were feeling good about our new home and were excited to share our good fortune during the upcoming Thanksgiving weekend—we were about to foster some rescues.

It was late afternoon, the Wednesday before Thanksgiving, when we arrived at the rescue. We had been laughing and joking on the way there that we would be giving our new home a holiday blessing. We had no idea how true that would be.

As we stood in the corral, watching the dogs play, we wondered who would be assigned to us. The director and my husband started chatting about "the usual" rescue subjects, like intakes and adoptions. I tuned them out, watching our son until I noticed, out of the corner of my eye, the director taking my husband by his hand and leading him back into the main office. Unconsciously registering only a small concern, I returned my focus to my young son as he tried to pick out, from the dozens of dogs, the one he wanted to care for. He was narrowing his choice down to a tiny, bowlegged Basset Hound.

A short time later my husband came back into the corral. Quietly reaching for my hand, he whispered, "We have to talk."

I knew this sentence; I had heard it from his lips in the same tone five times before. It always involved four legs and a happily wagging tail, along with a great deal of slobbering kisses. I looked up at him and saw in front of me the world's tallest boy, his crystal clear, blue, twinkling eyes promising me he would walk and feed the dog he found. As a small, familiar smile crossed my face, he could hardly control his delight.

"Okay, which one is it?" I asked, looking around and trying to guess, knowing in my heart the dog he wanted was not here in Chaos Park.

Leading, or I should say, pulling me by my hand out into the busy office area, David said, "He's out here." The director smiled and winked at me, knowing before I did (as was always the case) that a perfect fit had been made. She was "gifted" that way.

The dog, Berringer, had more bare spots and calluses than any dog should have. He was so thin his spine showed, accenting his rib and hip bones like they were accessories (from what I could tell they were all he owned). In some places fleas had chewed him down to the raw skin, and I wasn't convinced he would even make it through the weekend. Nevertheless, I thought, "Okay. I make him cookies and fatten him like a Christmas goose. I can do this."

"Well, it's only for the weekend," I said, knowing as the words came out of my mouth, it was forever. Berringer's sad, dull eyes told me he knew it, too, as I caught a glimpse of hope and happiness in them. To sweeten the deal, the rescue threw in Hoagie, the Basset Hound my son liked.

As the story goes, 11-year-old Berringer had found himself at the county shelter, no longer needed or loved. The owner came in when called about Berringer, but not to retrieve his old pal. I was told that instead Berringer sat watching sadly as his "best friend" demanded his electric collar but refused to take his dog. When he made a scene, the police were called, and the owner was forced to leave empty-handed. A kindly clerk then took it upon himself to call Labrador Retriever Rescue of Cincinnati (LRRoC), knowing they take all Labs, even old "un-adoptables." The volunteers, vets, and staff at Eastgate Animal Hospital (where LRRoC is based) all have room in their hearts for underdogs, and Berringer was definitely that.

So for the weekend our family was to be five—the three original members plus Berringer and Hoagie. At home, we inspected our new housemates more closely, which made us realize how horrible "Bear's" life must have been. When we touched him, he would shiver, being allowed in the house was a shock, and treats were completely unknown. He didn't understand carpeting and doggy beds either, so we first started him with a towel on the floor, and we plumped it up daily until he got the idea of a bed.

As predicted, our "weekend" of fostering ran long. It took weeks of continuous bathing for the water to run clean. I took pictures of him every day to mark his progress and my love, until one day, when I took an exceptional picture of him, I jokingly said, "High-five." Can you believe that Bear put up his paw and slapped mine? My husband found me weeping, holding and loving Bear. That evening as our whole "family" sat in front of the fireplace, where a warm fire burned away the snowy night, I questioned humanity: "How could someone teach Bear high-five and then ditch him?"

My husband just shook his head and scratched Bear's neck. Smiling broadly and gazing into Bear's golden eyes, he said, "It's their loss and our holiday blessing."

Berringer just smiled back, knowing, I am sure, exactly what was being said. His tail was now big and thick, and it banged away, hitting the table hard with enthusiasm and love. I had to laugh. After all, it didn't matter anymore, and especially not to Berringer because he was home and happy and his life was filled with love and warmth. There would be no more nights in the rain and cold, alone in the dark. Now he was part of our pack.

It's a year later now. Bear, or Care Bear as we call him, sleeps at my feet, free from most of the emotional and physical pains of yore, fur thick and full, snoring gently on a soft, comfortable doggy bed. His thoughtful eyes are clouded with cataracts so I am his eyes now, and when I'm not there to guide him, one of my many other rescues steps in. They slowly walk him though the backyard, keeping him safely away from the pool and stairs. They lie with him on cool fall nights, keeping him warm. They take turns sleeping with him, so he never has to sleep alone again.

I have learned from Berringer, my wonderful Bear, that even when things are the absolute worst, they can quickly change for the better. And maybe, just maybe, there is someone out there watching over us, making sure we get our holiday blessing.

 *Tammy Weiss*

A Wagging Achievement

A dog can express more with his tail in seconds than his owner can express with his tongue in hours.

Author Unknown

My husband and I thought we had it made in our little house with our two Labbies. Both our Yellow Lab, Huckleberry (aka "The Boss"), and our Black Lab, Bettis (aka "The Bus"), had been born in the country and handpicked at just eight weeks old.

Huckleberry came into our unsuspecting and naive dog-less lives like a hurricane, eating and chewing everything in sight. She slept only when her little body finally couldn't go anymore, and then she'd drop like a narcoleptic. Puppy school helped to train her...and us.

Huckleberry came with us to get our second dog. She picked Bettis, who happened to be the biggest dog in the litter. A rapidly growing, gentle giant just happy to be petted, Bettis became Huckleberry's main attraction, taking some of the heat off us exhausted new doggie parents. These two dogs never have known hardship: just twice daily walks; ongoing training; trips to the dog park, the beach, and the river; doggie swimming pools in the backyard; and endless chewies, pettings, and love. Any behavioral issues that came up were only the result of growing pains.

We had considered getting a third dog after a few foster dogs had come and gone. In fact, like a mother who yearns for another baby, I don't think I had a 'stopping mechanism' in me at that time; I was sure we'd adopt a few more over the course of the next few years.

Then a little, brown tornado flew into our path. Tahoe, aka "Little Bug," a six-month-old Brown Labbie with a curly tail, arrived as a nervous, little foster dog. We weren't sure if Bettis, now a good 50 pounds bigger than Tahoe, was going to accept another boy in the house. In fact, we thought Tahoe would become an appetizer. But Bettis let Tahoe know, in the ways that dogs do, that Tahoe was the lowest on the totem pole, but he would happily be Tahoe's big brother. Within two hours of his arrival, we decided Tahoe was the missing piece to our family puzzle. We adopted him within a week, and thus began the long journey to help him overcome his past.

Tahoe was abandoned when his owner was evicted from his home. In the shelter he was so ridden with anxiety that they thought it best he go to a foster home. His fear did not allow him to sleep more than five minutes; he'd jump up at any noise, crying and looking out the window—presumably for the owner who never returned. When we'd go outside, he'd dive bomb the windows, desperately trying to get out so he wouldn't be left again. He ate so fast that we had to start feeding him in a muffin tray with water-coated food to slow him down. He stole apples and bread off the counters if he was hungry and pulled on the leash like a wild boar when we walked.

However, as days turned into weeks and weeks into months, Tahoe caught the hang of our routine, and little by little, he calmed down. He stopped freaking when he saw us go outside and instead just nervously paced back and forth in the window until we came back in. Finally he'd sleep in the window with one eye open as we hung outside for a bit. He became a good little walker, hardly pulling on his leash, and he told us when he was ready to sleep like a big boy with his brother and sister on dog beds instead of in his crate.

The biggest milestone came just a few months ago when he started wagging his tail. Not a big deal for most dogs but for Tahoe a breakthrough. He was finally relaxed enough to have time to be happy. Day by day, his tail wags became bigger, more confident, and more frequent. He even discovered the tennis ball that had been flying past him for a year as his sister endlessly chased it. Now Tahoe even retrieves the ball and is learning to catch. After being unsure of our doggie pool, he tentatively gets in and starts splashing around. His favorite thing, though, is to cuddle up with us in the morning. He flops next to us and rolls over on his back for a belly rub while gently licking our faces, secure in knowing a walk and then breakfast comes next.

Tahoe turns two on Saturday. He's a survivor, and he'll always have fight in him to protect himself and his pack. But his little heart is now full of love, and he knows he is safe, part of *our* pack, and in his forever home. "The three amigos" have become inseparable. Huckleberry is busy raising her two little brothers and bossing them around. Bettis is thrilled to nurture his big sister and brother, always reminding Tahoe that he is the upper classman. Tahoe loves being the baby and is eager to please us all. We take full pleasure in watching them grow up and seeing how close their bonds have become.

It seems we have all come to peace with our roles. We feel privileged to celebrate Tahoe's incremental achievements (like tail wagging), but we are especially excited to say, "Happy Birthday to our Little Bug," who is reveling in his second puppyhood. I have no wish now for a fourth dog. You think I'm telling a white lie? Well, our hearts are always open and ready, so I could be. We'll just wait and see what life brings our way. For now though, we are a family of six (including our cat), and these three crazy Labbies keep us busy, broke, and blessed.

 *Warren and Sarah Guenther*

Life with Labs

Not the Brightest Brick in the Wall: Lucia seemed a good name for this girl, but within 12 hours I found that Lucifer was more fitting. This was a dog with a spirit too big for her 100-pound body. Once she ran into my neighbor's brick wall so hard that she knocked herself out. I had to carry that monstrous dog home, praying she didn't regain consciousness until we were safely inside the yard, with the gate locked. And when she did not come to immediately, I was afraid she was dead! No lie. -*Kimberly Tenai*

Brad is My Chew Toy: Casey, Yellow Lab, was a wild child and she chewed. A lot. Everything, in fact. Brad's Italian biking shoe. Brad's Blackberry. Brad's Bluetooth headset. Oh, Wild Child, *I think I love you.* Brad, on the other hand, is busy hiding his belongings! -*Kimberly Tenai*

Living With

After Hurricane Katrina passed, Franklin County Animal Shelter went down to New Orleans from Ohio to bring back six dogs. All were adopted except Katie, a 12-year-old Black Labrador with mammary cancer. The shelter vets gave her two months to live and advertised her story on the front page of their website, hoping to find someone who could provide "doggie hospice."

Katie's story left me wondering how this poor creature had survived the hurricane, only to be left to die of cancer alone in a shelter. I wasn't going to let that happen, so I phoned the Director and was touched by the compassion the staff had for this dog. If I could just give Katie a peaceful place to stay and be loved, the shelter would cover her medical bills.

It was October when I brought Katie home. That Halloween, I dressed her up in a red devil dog costume, and she sat on the porch with me waiting for all the trick-or-treaters. The kids loved and petted her as they came for candy, and Katie enjoyed the attention.

For almost a year Katie was happy and very playful. She befriended my other two Labs and two cats, and truly became a part of our family. On our daily walks Katie would bark at each passing dog, happily saying, "Look at me and my family!" She was the sweetest dog, and even though losing her to cancer broke my heart, I felt fortunate to share 11 great months with her. During that time, she was not *dying* of cancer—she was *living* with it.

The main thing I learned from Katie's story is the importance of spaying. I always knew spaying prevented pregnancy but came to learn it also helps prevent mammary (breast) cancer. It can even help if done later in life on dogs that have been bred, like Katie. Though it's too late for Katie, may the story of her death help extend the lives of others.

Lori Beattie

Aiden's Eyes

A iden came to live with us when he was six months old. I don't know if it was destiny, timing, or a well-devised plan that he became the third Labrador to steal our hearts. I first met Aiden when he arrived at Labrador Retriever Rescue of Cincinnati (LRRoC) at the tender age of eight weeks. I was making many trips to the animal hospital where they are based, desperately trying to figure out what was wrong with our female Labrador, Rosie. As I was waiting for the results of Rosie's x-rays one day, Roncy, the rescue director, said, "Hey, Julie, you have to see our newest baby boy."

Roncy held him close and then handed him to me. There he was, a timid, beautiful, gimpy, little baby boy. His eyes gleamed with compassion, emotion, and sensitivity—he was truly a special Lab. I hugged him, kissed his head, and handed him back to Roncy.

For the next few weeks I was consumed with taking care of Rosie. Sam, our oldest Labby, knew Rosie was sick, and he seemed to be heartbroken that he couldn't fix her. There were many days when he stood next to her and simply licked her head. Sam and Rosie were best friends; if a dog can have a soulmate, Rosie was Sam's.

Each time I brought Rosie to the hospital I checked on baby Aiden. The doc surmised Aiden had been stepped on when he was very young, crushing his front left leg and subsequently causing it to stop growing. He endured two major surgeries and received miraculous care from orthopedic surgeon Dr. Schrader, Roncy, and the wonderful staff at the hospital who cared for baby Aiden day and night. He couldn't walk, he ached from the external fixator bolted into his little leg, he had to wear the dreaded cone, and all the while he was experiencing the normal "growing pains" of teething and having too much energy that a growing Lab pup goes through.

As Rosie's condition worsened, we knew that her time with us was ending. The day we said goodbye to Rosie, Aiden came into our lives yet another time when Roncy brought Aiden into the lobby to see us. She looked at Anne, our youngest daughter, and said, "I know it doesn't help much, but you can hold the puppy if you want to." Aiden was now a four-month-old boy, still in a cast and the silly cone, now growing impatient with his situation. Anne and I took turns holding him and holding back our tears for our poor Rosie. I kissed Aiden's head again, and he looked at me with the most beautiful brown eyes I had seen. As we left that day, Roncy said, "You know, Aiden will need a home this summer."

I remember specifically saying, "Thanks, Roncy, but no thanks."

A few weeks passed, and we all missed Rosie terribly. Her passing was especially hard on her buddy, Sam. I checked the Lab rescue website daily, hoping to find him a companion. Finally I emailed Roncy, asking about a female who needed fostering. Roncy responded that she wouldn't be a good match for Sam. She then said, "Aiden is out of his cast and is at a swim therapy class today. He really needs to be with a family. Do you want to foster him?"

I asked everyone at home. Though my husband and daughters were eager to foster Aiden, we all had our doubts about making him a permanent member of the family. Nevertheless, we took him in and Aiden soon grew on all of us.

There were no fireworks when Aiden and Sam first met, but Sam instantly knew that he had a job…it was time to train this new pup. Sam helped Aiden learn how to run, jump, and swim within the first few days at our house. I still didn't really plan to adopt Aiden, but Sam seemed to have taken a shine to him, so what was I do?

My husband soon began to affectionately call him "Little Man" and gave him daily lectures about growing up to be a big boy like Sam. Anne became Aiden's personal chew toy. She liked him, as Aiden was learning to be a playful pup, but

Anne was still holding out for "her girl Genevieve." Macy, our older daughter, nicknamed Aiden "Nugget." She carried him around the house, every day questioning me about his adoption. She was soon leaving for Ecuador, and her plea to know if Aiden would be ours when she returned pulled at my heartstrings. So with Roncy's blessing, Aiden became a permanent member of our family.

Aiden has continued to amaze everyone with his physical abilities. His leg will never be perfect, and we know there will be battles down the road with arthritis and other issues, but he has become a real dog. He is a typical running, jumping, counter surfing Lab with a huge heart who still wants to be held like a baby, despite the fact that he is the size of a miniature horse. Aiden and Anne have become best friends. He snuggles each night with her on the couch and she wipes his face with a towel after he swims. He shares Shredded Wheat with Dad and Sam each morning.

So the book that truly began with Sam nearly ten years ago and continued with our dear, sweet Rosie, has a new chapter on our special boy Aiden. But it doesn't end there...

In January, Roncy called with unexpected news, "Julie, I have your girl, come see her tonight." This time I didn't hesitate. She was beautiful. She looked at me with her piercing eyes, I looked at her, I kissed her head, and I adopted her. The boys now have a sister and Anne has her girl, Genevieve. Aiden is now the teacher. He has taught her to run, jump, and counter surf. Sam helps when he feels like it, but most days I think he tells Aiden that this one is his job!

Black Labradors always catch my attention. I think it is the intensity in their eyes. Sam, Rosie, Aiden, and Genevieve have wonderful eyes that tell many stories. I didn't truly understand this until I met Aiden, who helped me grieve for Rosie, befriended Sam when he was lonely, and now is teaching Genevieve what it means to be a Lab in our family. It's not his injuries that make him special; it's the look in his eyes and the depth behind them.

 *Julia Ayers*

Hugo in Stereo

Julie (Mom):

I have always been known as the "cat lady" (we have three), and for over twenty years I have resisted my husband's pleas to add a dog to the mix. What if he's rough with the kids? What if he doesn't like the cats? Where will he stay when we go on vacation? But when our three beautiful daughters joined my husband on his quest for a Lab, I finally, wholeheartedly, gave in. If you can't beat them, join them, right?

Lexi (Daughter):

We got our Lab, Hugo, from OKI Lab Rescue. He is about three years old and very happy living with my parents, my sisters, and me.

Hugo was rescued from the wild with another Lab. He has a sad past, and it surprises us that he shows no signs of aggression to anybody. Whoever had Hugo before he either ran away or was set free, mistreated him. By *mistreated* I mean he was chained in a backyard where he could only wander around on cement. We know this because the pads on his paws were cracked badly. He also was shot in the foot with a BB gun. We are absolutely sure of this because during the one of the first check-ups, the vet had noticed there was a large bump on his back paw. My dad thought it was a type of cancer, and we asked the vet about it. We were all very relieved to find out that it was not cancer, but at the same time we were saddened that somebody would be heartless enough to shoot a dog. His suffering finally ended when the OKI Lab Rescue took Hugo in and placed him with a great foster parent.

Julie:

Hugo's bio went something like this: *"...a rogue who will con you into letting him out for a potty break when he really only wants to play fetch."* What an understatement that was! Hugo's so obsessed with fetching tennis balls he has "taught" the neighbors on both sides of our fenced-in yard how to play with him. He's dug a little divot by the fence where he deposits the ball—one on each neighbor's side! They throw the ball over the fence, and our tireless retriever brings it right back to the divot, like a fetch/mini-golf combo.

Lexi:

If one of us is playing ball with him, he brings it back and drops it at our feet. Then he does what our family calls "puppy face." This is when he puts up his ears and cocks his head to the side. With that he always gets his way.

I play golf, and sometimes practice in the backyard. Since our backyard is not the type of yard you would practice hitting golf balls in, I hit the tennis ball. Of course, Hugo goes and fetches it. This is probably his all-time favorite game.

Julie:

Lexi, Haley, and Cami refer to him as their brother and like all good sisters, introduced him to the wonderful world of dress-up. Hugo found out that a size 12, girl's tu-tu, a monochromatic purple sweater, beads, and a veil create a rather becoming look on a 95-pound, male Yellow Lab. Tolerant to a fault, he actually seems to enjoy it. Did I mention his toenail polish often matches the outfit?

Lexi:

Hugo loves the cats, especially Spooky. It was only days before Halloween when we adopted Spooky from our cousins, and with her being a black cat, Spooky was the perfect name. Hugo took this in an odd way. Instead of chasing her, he treats her like a baby and "mothers" her. Spooky and Hugo are now inseparable.

Julie:

A bath with Hugo results in Spooky looking more like a little drowned rat than a cat. Not even the insides of her ears are missed! If we crate Hugo, Spooky's right there beside him. As odd as a couple can get, they truly do love each other. I just wonder if Hugo's grateful, caring spirit comes from once having known a harsh way of life before being rescued from the streets.

On the other hand, Hugo is intimidated by our Garfield-looking cat, Ringo, who takes it upon himself to put Hugo in line with a loud hiss from time to time. Poor Hugo usually whimpers, cowers, and creeps away from the fierce feline.

After being a part of the family for over two years, Hugo's bio reads something like this: *"Gentle, yet goofy; active and fond of chewing; a protector and a couch potato; stubborn and a character; Mother Theresa and Clarabell the Clown (simultaneously!); cat and gerbil kisser but hater of the vacuum cleaner; best friend and confidante."* What is most true about him is that he is pure, unconditional love and loyalty personified. I could never have imagined the joy this "cat lady" would have missed out on had we not adopted Hugo.

Lexi:

We all love Hugo very much.

 *Lexi & Julie Ford*

Do You Know This Dog?

T he ad in the local newspaper caught our attention while we were having breakfast: *"Do You Know This Dog?"* The handsome black Lab was found as a stray at City Market and had been at the Aspen Animal Shelter for two weeks. The ad caught my eye because our previous Lab had passed in December after a long illness, and we were very lonely for a dog. We called the shelter and learned that "Buddy" was still there and available for adoption.

At the shelter it was love at first sight, but the shelter staff insisted we take him out for the day to make sure we like him. We were in Aspen on a fly-fishing trip, so we headed to one of our favorite spots, Woody Creek Bridge on the Roaring Fork River. As soon as we arrived, a tennis ball floated up to shore—it was "shorely" a sign! Buddy was *our* dog now, and his new name would be Woody.

Woody was "Mr. Manners" the whole day. In fact, he was so well-behaved, we started thinking he must be the trained companion of a wealthy Aspenite, who would suddenly appear and claim him. He sat at the river's edge and waited until we invited him into the water. He stayed close and never barked. We couldn't believe someone wasn't missing such a great dog.

When we returned to the shelter to adopt him, we talked about his past. They told us seasonal workers or ski bums probably abandoned him at the end of season, as is often the case in resort towns. We didn't have to worry about someone claiming him because he had no tags or microchip. "Buddy" was officially *our* "Woody" now.

Woody seemed unsure of what was happening but happy to be with us. Nevertheless, after a few weeks we began seeing signs of separation anxiety. Maybe he was worried that he would be abandoned again. The first time we left him alone in the house he tore down the blinds in the living room window. The next time we put him in the back yard, and he tried to pull the boards off the cedar fence.

With no other obvious option we began taking Woody with us everywhere or hiring a dogsitter when he had to be left home. He went to doggy daycare when we went to work, and when we had to attend a family wedding out of state, we boarded him at the same daycare facility. He did fine during the day but chewed holes all around the top of his big, galvanized aluminum water bucket the first night, resulting in a broken tooth.

We decided Woody needed a constant companion, so we started searching for a second dog—we liked being a two dog family anyway. We soon found our sweet Golden, Claire Bear, put in a doggy door for them, and held our breath. Her companionship was just what the doctor ordered! Woody took Claire under his wing, we were able to leave them home alone, and all of our problems were solved. Or so we thought...

A while later we all went on another fishing trip to Woody's old home territory. One afternoon Don hooked a nice trout, and Woody was instantly in the water. We were so shocked—where was Mr. Manners of Aspen? As if wanting to drive home a point, Woody then grabbed the fish and took off! Horrified, we caught him and released fish, which didn't seem hurt. Here we were, meeting a new challenge, another side of Woody we hadn't seen before. Woody now goes crazy when he sees fish rising or sees us catching one. (And yes, we do feed him.)

That same trip, we made the mistake of briefly leaving Woody and Claire in the truck while we fished at a certain hot spot. When we returned to the truck and opened the doors, we just stood there, stunned. Woody had ripped the leather interior to shreds—the seats, the headliner, everything. Maybe there was a reason someone had left him behind. No matter, we still love him, and we won't make *that* mistake again.

Woody continues to evolve. He is now very vocal at times. He barks at us to say, "Throw the ball!" or, "Let's go for a walk!" Other times he is relaxed and snuggly. I've actually had people say, "That's the mellowest Lab I've ever seen." If only they knew...

We probably spoiled Woody too much in the beginning when he was so nervous and insecure, but in any case, this is his forever home and we love him. "Do You Know This Dog?" We do for now, but who knows what future antics he'll dream up. We don't care and we wouldn't change a thing. One thing is for sure - he's *our* Woody!

 *Mary and Don Miceli*

Life with Labs

Indecent Exposure: We laugh when we see fat Molly running along her fence at her new home nearby, and the whole family howls when we remember me chasing one runaway chocolate girl down the street in my underwear! Which one was it? Nutmeg? Lissy? Mokalata? I don't know, but I am certain the garbage men remember! *-Kimberly Tenai*

The Lifeguard: When I met Dekie, he was an obese Yellow Lab—nothing like my perfect Bailey. I adopted him anyway and came to find he was so much more than his unsocialized awkwardness let on. I often think back to the first time I took Dekie swimming with Bailey. Dekie thought Bailey was struggling and immediately jumped in, grabbing Bailey's neck in his mouth, attempting to drag him to shore. I was equally mesmerized by Dekie's act of love and saddened that couldn't even make the distinction between play and distress. As they say, though, love heals all wounds, and these days Dekie's tail is in chronic motion as he has finally learned from Bailey how to be a dog. *-Caryl Kerns*

Jail Dog

*C*harles is serving 15 to 50 years at the Madison County Correctional Institute in London, Ohio, but for one Yellow Lab named Chase his crimes and sentence didn't matter. Charles would become his teacher, life saver (literally), and his very best friend.

It was hard not to miss the bony, six-month-old dog as he sniffed empty burger wrappers in a fast food restaurant parking lot. Chase, as he would later be named by Charles, weighed just 29 pounds (at least 30 pounds underweight), and as if that weren't bad enough, someone had used him for target practice. He had either a bullet or BB lodged in the middle of his forehead.

An employee of the restaurant called the Humane Society of Madison County about the stray hanging around outside.

Already overcrowded, they were able to place Chase in a cell dog program called A Fresh Start. This program is a partnership between the Madison County Correctional Institute, their inmates who have exhibited excellent behavior, and a local Humane Society. Chase would become Charles' cellmate for two months while Charles trained him and kept a daily journal of his progress. Charles writes:

When I first got him, I didn't think he would make it, but I didn't give up on him like the people who left him. I hand fed him for about a week, three times a day. I had to feed him slowly because I didn't want his weight to be put on too fast.

As Chase got stronger their bond grew:

Chase pulls at my heart. He needs everything; trust, love, and a caring person. I want him to know that I am not the same person that had him before, that I WILL NOT HURT HIM.

Charles began training Chase, knowing within a month or two he would have to say goodbye. With positive reinforcement Chase learned quickly.

He knows sit, stay, come, off, up, kennel, out, take it, drop it, and I am still working on heel. He still has a lot of puppy in him, and it is hard for him to heel all the time. He also knows shake. Man, I love this dog!

The Fresh Start program is a two-way street, helping both dogs and inmates. Chase got the love, nurturing, and training he needed while Charles gained self-respect.

I have been in a lot of programs to better myself but let me tell you, this one has changed me more than all of them together. I have never in my life been proud of anything I have done or will do. I am now!

Two months and 30 pounds later, Chase was ready to leave for his new adopted home with us. It was bittersweet for Charles; it always is. He has cared for, trained, and then had to say goodbye to Chase and 16 other dogs, who were fortunate enough to pass his way. My husband and I left with a smart, confident, and exuberant dog named Chase, along with the original journal and a parting note to us from Charles.

I have never in my life really cared about anything or anyone. I never felt the love that I feel with the dogs that I help. Every one that I train means so much to me. I remember them all. I hope you like Chase as much as I do. He will soon be your best pal like he is with me. Take good care of him, and I am sure you will fall in love with him, too. Tell him I love and care about him, that I had to help more of his friends out there that also need help. Please keep me updated, and let me know how he is doing from time to time.

Thank you, Charles

It has been almost three months since we adopted Chase, "Charlie Chase" as we call him. Going through the Humane Society, we pen monthly letters to Charles from Chase, recounting his big and small adventures. He always starts his letters with "Dear Dad…" After all, Charles was the first real family he ever had.

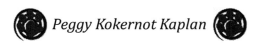 *Peggy Kokernot Kaplan*

Porter Pride

I'll be honest with you. We have had our challenges with Porter.

The sign at the Portland Humane Society said, "Lab/ Border Collie mix." He was the last one left of his littermates, a four-month-old, little, black puppy. With the paperwork completed I gathered him up in my arms with a blanket, and we headed to our car. Off we went, tears welling up in my eyes, so happy to have a new member of our family. We've always had a dog, so we looked forward to the years ahead, prepared for the events to come... So we thought.

That calmness Porter fooled us with on the "get acquainted" visit was short-lived. He soon became a whirlwind of nonstop activity. Unlike a lot of puppies, he never seemed to have a slow period. He rarely took a nap and would never sit still for petting. Porter was in constant motion.

Porter loved to chew; his only selection criterion was that it fit in his mouth. Most of the things he chose were fairly harmless, and socks were his favorite. However, he crossed the line when he chewed up our son's expensive tooth guard and our daughter's cell phone. When he ate my Nike+ GPS device that tracks my training miles, I thought, "At least we will always know where he is." We had to watch him like a hawk, not out of our sight for more than a few seconds.

I knew there had to be a way to control this happy-go-lucky guy so Porter became my personal challenge, and I was determined to reach him. First on the agenda was making sure he got plenty of exercise—two walks a day plus plenty of play-time in the yard.

We had good luck with a trainer for our Border Collie so we looked her up for Porter. The classes began and so did the slow transformation. He quickly learned the names of all twelve of his toys and would search until he found just the one we had asked him to get. He loved a challenge and was focused when given a job to do, so we started searching out other activities for him. He was about six months old when we signed him up for agility. He thought that was great fun, but we could not spend our whole day at the agility barn with him. Once back at home he was back to his old trouble: barking for attention, jumping, and getting into things. We still could not have him out of our sight for more than a minute. We kept at it though, trying to be consistent. Getting him out for exercise was paramount.

When Porter was around eight months old we took him to Dock Dogs, thinking he could become a champion competitor. He seemed to have all of the traits to do well— he was very toy driven, loved to jump, and loved the water— which he proved to me every time I watered the garden, jumping as high as he could to get the spray from the hose. Well, Porter decided that standing at the edge of the puppy dock and barking at the floating toy was more fun than actually jumping in to get it. Maybe when he gets a little older we will revisit this activity.

We continued with obedience classes and daily training on obedience and tricks, which he loved to do. Somewhere along the line we noticed something else was happening. We found ourselves bragging to friends about Porter, telling funny little stories about something he had done that week. We realized just how much we were falling in love with this crazy dog and his happy-go-lucky nature.

We started seeing progress, a light at the end of the tunnel. Porter was actually sitting still for petting, if only for a moment. Then things started taking off for Porter. We entered him into a dog competition for tricks and were so proud when he won first place with play dead, roll over, take a bow, and then a high-five finale.

We did the unthinkable next... We started leaving him in the house alone for a few hours at a time, to see how he would do. Amazingly the house survived, nothing was bothered. Could our crazy dog possibly be left alone while we were at work now? We gave it a shot. With my husband making it home for lunch most days, Porter made the transition from the big 6' x 12' kennel in the garage to being left at home all day! In our eyes this was nothing short of miraculous.

Porter is almost three now, and we have done many new activities with him. He goes running with me on a waist-leash and stays nicely at my side. He waits his turn in the morning to get his teeth brushed. But his most favorite thing in the world (besides eating) is running on the treadmill. Saying "treadmill" to Porter is like asking another dog if they want to go for a ride in the car. Like a cartoon character his feet start running on the kitchen floor faster than he can move. He darts up the stairs to the workout room, jumps onto the treadmill, and barks until we can get it going for him. We even do family workouts: Porter on the treadmill, my husband on the stair climber, and me on my bike trainer.

Porter is still a work in progress as he turns three, but we could not love him more and are so proud of the dog he has become. We have just recently begun the process of training him as a Rescue Dog, knowing Porter is destined for something great. Whether dock dog, rescue dog, or just the best family dog that anyone could have, we could not imagine life without our wild and crazy Porter. Who knows what he will do next?

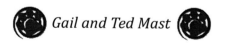 *Gail and Ted Mast*

What's in a Name?

S aying we foster a lot of dogs is an understatement. My family of three has saved 27 lives in four years. We're not saints, miracle workers, or veterinarians; we're just people who have opened our door to dogs in need and to the love, joy, and chaos that dog rescue brings.

We only fostered yellow or chocolate females as our first rescue, Feki, a black male, would not tolerate other males, and he hated other black dogs. Feki was 12 years old when we lost him last summer, but as my heart broke, we keep fostering.

Before Feki passed, when Lucas, my son, was three, we had a ritual that highlights the best of animal rescue. At night, when I tucked Lucas beneath his blanket, the following conversation would ensue:

Lucas: "I love you, Mommy."

Me: "I love you, too."

Lucas: "I love Daddy."

Me: "I love your daddy, too."

Lucas: "I love Feki."

Me: "I love Feki, too."

Lucas: "I love Mercredi." (Not forgetting our kitty.)

Me: "I love Mercredi, too."

Lucas would then pause for a moment. He would begin, "And I love…" Often he stopped. He would think. And then he would tentatively ask, "What's the brown dog's name again?"

Sometimes I would have to pause a moment and think, as well. What is the new dog's name? But I would love her anyway. And most importantly, I love having a house filled with kindness and a little bit of craziness, and a child who is learning to love the creatures in our world.

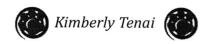 *Kimberly Tenai*

A Victim of "Good Intentions"

This is the story of Ariel, a puppy bred in Michigan by someone with good intentions—a puppy destined to be shown...if she "turned out." Ariel, however, stayed petite and was too small to compete with other black females in the serious world of AKC dog shows, so Ariel's breeder sold her as a pet.

At 15 months old, Ariel was purchased by two young women who thought she'd make a great present for their father, a man who was alone and recently divorced. For many in this situation a dog can be just the thing, but this divorcé was also suffering from a range of debilitating psychological conditions, making it very hard for him to function in society (let alone care for a dog). The daughters, perhaps confusing the dog with the mythological *Archangel Ariel of Healing and New Beginnings*, hoped she would rid their father of his loneliness and depression. It wasn't long, though, before their good intentions also went awry.

It must be said that usually when an adult really *wants* a dog he finds one on his own. Lucky "gift" puppies quickly find themselves in new homes; unlucky ones, sadly, are sometimes tossed into the streets. Ariel was no exception—receiving less and less attention as the father's condition worsened, she soon found herself in need of a new home. Fortunately the father's minister stepped in and, with the man's blessing, contacted a Lab rescue. The rescue volunteers evaluated Ariel, and after determining that she did, indeed, have the wonderful, gregarious personality typical of the breed, they agreed to try and find her a home.

The first plan was for Ariel to stay with her owner, who could then participate in the process of choosing the appropriate applicant for her. Sadly the rescue quickly realized he wasn't able to return phone calls, so they moved her into foster care with Roseanne and Kevin Maloney of Lakewood, Ohio.

It didn't take long, however, for Matthew and Jennifer Keefer to discover Ariel on the rescue website, and immediately they were smitten. After losing their first rescued Labrador Retriever, Charlotte, to cancer, they knew they wanted to give another rescue dog a forever home. Ariel seemed just perfect.

Some might think that travelling the four hours from State College, PA, to Cleveland, OH, to meet a dog is crazy, but it wasn't for Matthew and Jennifer. The only potential hitch was their quirky, dog-loving cat, Tucson, the king of their house. The couple couldn't bring him on the road trip, so they were left guessing if the animals would get along.

On meeting Ariel, Matthew and Jennifer absolutely wanted to be a part of the little Lab's life. So with the Maloney's approval, they made the journey back to Pennsylvania with their new dog. Despite their optimism, though, Ariel almost got herself a one-way ticket back to Ohio after only a few days. Like her namesake in the Shakespearian play "The Tempest," Ariel caused quite the upset for Tucson due to her natural inclination to chase him. He was brave, and tried to make friends with her, but continuously had to return to hiding.

The Keefers were heartbroken, but they couldn't make Tucson live with a dog who terrorized him. With no other clear choice, Jennifer called the rescue to make arrangements to return Ariel to Cleveland.

It was as if Ariel sensed the imminent four-hour drive, because she suddenly had a change of heart. The morning of the planned trip, the Keefers awoke to find Ariel and Tucson lying side-by-side in the hallway outside their bedroom door. Suddenly Ariel no longer wanted to eat Tucson, and they were best buds? It seemed a little fishy, but hey, whatever works.

Perhaps imperfect by dog show standards, Ariel is a darling dog who is truly a "sprite"—a blithe spirit of enormous good will. When not being teased by her feline brother Tucson, Ariel is busy performing tricks, swimming in the neighborhood stream, and indulging in lots of belly rubs. She can't wait for her daily walks (rain or shine), and flies around the house if the word "walk" is spoken out loud. Too many times a victim of good intentions, Ariel is home for good. Again happy, playful, and affectionate, she touches everyone around her with a sprinkle of spritely magic.

 *Jennifer Stingelin Keefer and Matt Keefer*

Surprise Inside

We enter the final chapter. Somehow in the last 24 hours your spindly legs stopped supporting your 100 pounds. Suddenly years of memories flood back, and in between my tears I laugh out loud.

We had an unconventional meeting. Who knew one could meet a dog online and, just as they say, when you least expect it love comes. It was a casual effort on my part, cruising through breeder's websites, ooh-ing and aah-ing at photos of beautiful and surely well-behaved dogs. All my prior dogs had been, umm, bordering on bizzarro behaviors; they all fit into the "goofball" category. But this time was going to be a concerted effort to find an older pal, one with exemplary traits—a turnkey dog. Chewing, digging, barking, and howling would never exist in this future older dog, only perfection.

The surprise came one day by way of the announcement: "You've got mail." It was an obscure, mysterious note from someone, mentioning the availability of an older Lab with no details other than a phone number. The area code was some faraway place, but my interest was bubbling. In an instant, fingers were dialing the numbers.

The quiet voice on the other end of the phone belonged to a carpenter, who spoke of his client's dog. He said the dog was big, beautiful, and lonely. Buzz word. Thoughts racing, heart pounding, hearing him ask if I would call the dog's owner. But how could I, when they didn't even know their carpenter had become a matchmaker for their dog?

We settled on the carpenter notifying his clients of his crafty plan, and only then would I make a call. On the phone he next day, the quiet voice said his part of the deal was done, and within an hour the arranged marriage had been completed. The lonely dog would fly here and be the ideal, hundred-pound, well-behaved dog they promised me.

While driving to the airport, expectations crept in. This dog would be the perfect Lab, and of course, I would be a model guardian. As the carrier was opened, though, a massive and wild, 130-pound creature charged out. A last ditch grab at his leash resulted in a shoulder-jerking trip around the parking lot, until he finally stopped. Snorting, growling. How could this be the dog I had imagined?

What a ride we have been on all these years: three trainers, surgeries galore, a plethora of medications, special diets, nonstop aggravations, irritations... Yet still my heart entwines with yours, every beat. You have been my friend, my therapist, another parent helping raise my son, and now I am resigned to entering the final chapter with you, calling you every nickname that rolls off my lips, hugging and kissing the days away.

Crackerjax, you're the best.

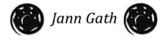 *Jann Gath*

Life with Labs

Fun and Dandy: Frightened by Fourth of July fireworks, Dandy was struck by a car. His fractured pelvis made walking difficult, and he was also diagnosed with Heartworm. A typical Lab, the necessary inactivity during his recovery didn't stop Dandy from having fun. Tennis balls, it turns out, can be an endless good time, even with no one to throw them. Dandy's game started with resting a ball on a low ledge in his "recovery room." He then waited until it rolled off, gleefully catching it to start the game again. Not alone in his amusement, Dandy's simple pleasure always brought a smile to our faces, too. *-Jan Thaman*

A Fox in the Garden

A Thoughtful Rescuer:

Once upon a time, a Labrador Retriever rescuer was called to evaluate some dogs in the Wayne County (Ohio) Humane Society's shelter. One was indeed a Labrador Retriever; the rescuer determined the temperament was fine and put the dog into her van for the trip back home. Then this rescuer did something she usually never did—she walked along the line of holding pens and looked at "other" dogs. What should she spot but a little, black, fox-like face peering out at her with sparkling, black eyes. It was a sweet, little puppy, though certainly NOT a purebred Lab. But fate was pulling the strings that day, and the rescuer took the little, black, fox-looking dog out of her pen and into a new life.

Fox did fine in foster care, but the folks who came to the Lab rescue were usually looking for a purebred dog. This was a challenge for Fox, and it took a while to find her family. But in the end it was worth the wait. *Just ask her...*

A Grateful Dog:

It seemed like I was at my foster mom's forever. It was a nice place, but I still wanted my very own family. I did my best to entertain happy-looking families that came to meet dogs, but for some reason they all passed me by.

Finally a family came just to see me, and I felt they were special. I let them pet me, and one of them even rubbed my tummy. I chased the toy they threw, but they still left without me. I couldn't figure out what I was doing wrong. I'd heard my foster mom tell them: "This is a very people-focused dog. This dog wants to retrieve." Isn't that what Lab people like?

Soon after, my foster mom took me and some other dogs to an adoption party. And that's when I spotted them...the family I met at my foster mom's house! They had come back to see me, and this time they took me home. I liked my new digs and sniffed every corner. They gave me a bath, and my new mom brushed me while cooing that I was very pretty. I liked her so much I started following her everywhere.

Everyone seemed so happy I'd arrived. They gave me a new name, Kelt, and I liked the sound of it. They put up a fence so I would have the whole yard to play in, but they really didn't need to worry—I was so delighted to be "home," I wasn't going anywhere.

My mom has a large vegetable garden, and every day she takes me there, introducing me to new things. She tells me what everything is as she picks parts of her many plants and puts them in a basket. Sometimes I even get to taste-test! I'll never forget the day she gave me a green bean. Boy, was that ever great! My tummy was in love, so I figured out how to get them all by myself—my mom still laughs about that for some reason. She also let me explore the garden patch, where I discovered a weird-looking green thing my mom called a "cuke." Now *that* was a remarkable treat!

To thank my mom for all the wonderful things she gives me, I have learned to keep various "critters" out of our yard. Before I arrived there were all sorts of them—bunnies, squirrels, moles—but I've been very busy and they now know not to come around. There is no way I am going to let them steal our vegetables!

After eating vegetables from the garden, my next favorite thing is playing Frisbee. I love to chase it and can catch it in the air. Better yet, though, is my floating Frisbee. My diving skills have earned me the nickname "the black torpedo" because I fly into the water after it. What a riot!

My family and I have just clicked. Since the day they brought me home, we have shared in happiness together. Their hugs tell me they are my own special family forever, and I am their best friend.

Kelt, translated to "human-speak" by Diane Valasek

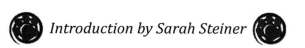 *Introduction by Sarah Steiner*

The Love of a Labrador

According to Greek myth, Penelope was the cousin of the infamous Helen of Troy, who launched a thousand ships, and the wife of Odysseus, the war hero who conquered Troy. In the traditional tale, while Helen and Odysseus were off having various adventures, Penelope was the ever-faithful wife, keeping the home fires burning. The name Penelope has come to signify a loyal, capable, and clever woman.

My Penelope story is not about a faithful woman who sat at home waiting for her man, but instead it is about an intelligent, beautiful, black English Lab who loyally helped me through some of my toughest times.

My friend and companion has had a sad, sad story from beginning to end. Penelope was part of a backyard breeder's brood and was kept constantly pregnant for the sake of profit. She and her male partner knew they were destined for a higher calling and kept trying to run away from their uncaring owner, but they were always caught and returned to their prison. One day they escaped and Penelope became a hit-and-run victim of a reckless driver.

Lying unconscious on the road with her male partner standing over her, a Good Samaritan rescued the pair and delivered them to a kind veterinarian. Fortunately the doctor recognized beauty in the two dogs and contacted the breeder to let her know he was caring for them. To his surprise the owner was furious and shouted, "I'm tired of those two getting out of their kennel—euthanize them!" The veterinarian refused her death order and had her sign the dogs over to him. The male went into a foster home, and after Penelope was treated and healed from her accident, she went into a Lab rescue facility.

Penelope and I met when I was searching for a Labrador Retriever to home school in service dog etiquette. She was interviewed with the plan that she would become my constant and personal assistant, and it really seemed to me that she wanted, and needed, a job. You see, for approximately 15 years I had been dealing with the challenges of Multiple Sclerosis (MS). I was still employed but my MS had become progressive, with headaches, clumsiness, and fatigue occurring more frequently on top of adjusting to life in a wheelchair. With all the emotions of blame, separation, and worthlessness constantly nagging at me, I began to realize that I needed help at so many different levels in order to remain employed.

My employer was not willing to hire a person to help in my office, so the better alternative was the assistance from a service dog. A canine companion who could maneuver around retrieving, holding, carrying, and helping me with daily activities would be an irreplaceable presence in my life.

It didn't take long for me to realize that Penelope's life before I met her was not that of a three-year-old, happy-go-lucky Labrador. She had to be trained on how to retrieve, and she did not know how to play, swim, or interact with other animals. Despite her low self-esteem, she was very smart, eager to please, and able to learn new tasks quickly.

After about six months of at-home training exercises and socialization sessions at shopping centers and restaurants, Penelope was ready to begin her short-lived career as a service dog. Her favorite task was to "Get the mail!" to my neighbors and coworkers delight. She would hold a mouthful of envelopes, catalogs, or memos tightly, until she knew I had a firm hold on them, at which time she would "drop it." She was a dedicated companion who was only distracted from her job by those who tried to love on her and didn't understand she was working.

With her help for four years, I was able to achieve greater independence and face new challenges. Her career ended because my career ended when the complications from the mix of surgeries and MS made it impossible for me to work away from my home. Even though she no longer heard the phrase, "It's time to go to work," she continued to retrieve anything that I asked her to get. She had the ability to understand the physical changes that were occurring to my body and modify the way she retrieved to meet my needs.

Stoicism, I believe, is a common trait of many Labrador Retrievers, and in Penelope's case, she carried it to a fault, never letting on she wasn't well. During one of my physical therapy sessions, while she was waiting, she vomited in the car. She then started consuming excessive amounts of water and would not eat. Even though she did not seem to be in pain, she was not her lively self. After inconclusive x-rays and blood tests, she ended up at an emergency animal hospital. Even though this episode occurred one year ago, I relive the emotions as if it happened yesterday: Penelope was diagnosed with cancer.

She had lymphoma and her liver was failing. She lived for four days through chemotherapy and steroid treatments, but on her last day she told me, by the look in her eyes, she wasn't going to make it. It was time to let her know that it was all right to let go of life. As the veterinarian was administering the lethal dose of anesthetic I held her, caressed her, and whispered, "It's ok, you can go to sleep," and soon her heart stopped beating.

Penelope taught me so much about the importance of life and death and unconditional love, just by watching and interacting with her. She learned she wasn't a failure and others recognized that she was full of love. Penelope's and my feelings of anger, blame, separation, and worthlessness began to diminish, and the feeling of being whole and connected increased together. I believe the benefits of

Penelope's higher service dog calling was not just for her or my sake, but for many others, too. On a daily basis people would stop us to chat and tell us their story about some time in their life when they experienced the love of a Labrador Retriever. Laughter over their silly antics, respect for their gentle and dedicated personalities, and tears were shed over the loss of a Labrador Retriever.

 *Paula Lang*

Something to Chew On

The search for Walter began when Abby, our first dog, started to seem lonely. Since Ben and I had always had two dogs, it was an easy decision to get a companion for her. I have a hard time looking at dogs online (they have these *"pick me"* faces, and I want to take them all home), so Ben was responsible for the search. He soon found Reggie, the perfect dog.

Reggie had been rescued from a backyard breeder. He was a Chocolate Lab and quite handsome. After growing attached to his picture, Ben and I were both disappointed to learn, however, that Reggie had already been spoken for. The rescue invited us to look at another dog who had waltzed in from the same backyard breeder instead. His name was Walter.

Walter was white with pink markings, undesirable traits in the breeding world of Labs. He was a big boy, too, because his owners used to just rip open a bag of food in a barn and let all their dogs fend for themselves. His markings and weight didn't matter to us, though. We finalized the adoption paperwork and took him home, expecting there would be *some* challenges. Boy, were we in for a surprise!

In the two years we've had Walter, he has eaten the following: the breezeway floor, siding on the house, two TV remotes, countless throw rugs, dish towels and towels, couch cushions, pillows, a coffee table, the bathroom floor, the carpet, and both papasan chairs. This chewing behavior is probably attributed to the fact that he grew up in a barn where he could chew anything.

Neglected dogs like Walter either really crave human affection or are standoffish. Walter chose affection. He is happiest when cuddling on our laps (our 95-pound lapdog) or sleeping beside us with his head on the pillow. His gentle disposition and ability to bring out the puppy in Abby made his chewing slightly easier to bear, and in time he finally finished his "eat everything" phase.

Our cats love him, Abby would be lost without him, and I can't imagine coming home without Walter's big, goofy face waiting to greet me.

 *Julie and Ben Sadler*

Rescue and Recovery

It started with an email: a friend of a friend saw a cute, female Chocolate Lab named "Godiva" at a county pound. She wouldn't last long there since she was limping, but she had a wonderful temperament. I met with a fellow rescuer who pulled her from the shelter and that is when "Godiva" became "Lilly." She seemed to like that name better; I know I did. She was *so* nice and *so* engaging—how did she come to be in the hands of the dog warden?

The next stop was the vet for a consultation. I could see that Lilly's left front leg looked wrong. The vet took x-rays and broke the bad news: Lilly needed corrective surgery to save her leg. They weren't sure if it had been broken and not repaired or if it was a birth defect, but either way she needed medical care. Since I had been through this type of thing before, I decided to continue fostering Lilly.

Our vet made a phone call, and we were set for a consult at Ohio State University's College of Veterinary Medicine in Columbus. It's about a 2½ hour drive, so Lilly and I got on the road early (lucky for me Lilly enjoys car rides). The exam confirmed that Lilly had a genetic birth defect that caused her left front leg to be 30 percent shorter than her right and the left front foot to be turned in 30 degrees. This defect was stressing her elbow and shoulder, which were already exhibiting arthritis. I was given two options: corrective surgery or waiting, the latter would probably require leg amputation once she stopped growing.

I had to wonder, was Lilly a throw-away dog because of her lameness? Probably. Maybe an unhappy puppy buyer unloaded her because they couldn't get any help from the breeder. Maybe there wasn't a reputable breeder and instead it was a pet store that wouldn't help. I guess it doesn't really matter except to those of us in rescue. We try to discover the underlying factors of why dogs like Lilly end up in rescue and in shelters. This knowledge helps us to educate the public to possibly prevent (or at least reduce) the number of dogs coming into rescue.

Our rescue group, Lake Erie Labrador Retriever Rescue, Inc. (LELRR), had some hard decisions to make. Fixing Lilly's leg would be expensive. Waiting would result in her losing a leg. As is true for most rescue groups, funds are limited, and we must decide whether to save one dog or twenty. I posed the question to the trustees: "Can we justify saving one dog when we might save twenty?" Their answer was, "Can we not?" Appointments were made, and Lilly went back to OSU.

To explain what Dr. Dyce did for Lilly would be a chapter in a medical book. The procedure is known as Osteogenesis Distraction using a Ring Fixator. By breaking one of the lower leg bones and then securing it with pins to several inter-connected circular braces, Dr. Dyce and his orthopedic team were able to straighten the leg and lengthen it. This procedure involved twisting and spreading these braces daily, by very small amounts, over a period of 4-6 weeks.

Lilly stayed at OSU for the entire period. We received daily updates and pictures from the students, and by all accounts she was a model canine citizen. At follow-up visits the staff would stop by to play with Lilly and comment on how nice she had been while she stayed there.

At last it was time to drive down and pick her up. Lilly would still need to have the brace on her leg and would need daily care to keep it clean. There was to be no running or jumping (this was the most difficult part of her recuperation) and only short walks on a leash for another 4-6 weeks. Lilly took it all in stride and seemed to revel in the attention.

After her final visit to OSU, Lilly was a free dog. She could run and jump and play and just be normal. Her left leg was almost the same length as the right one and was properly aligned. She wasted no time and became very good friends with the other dogs in our house, taking particular interest in Joey, another foster dog with a troubled history. She seemed to make an effort to help Joey understand what it is to live with people who won't hurt you. She helped Joey immensely with his rehabilitation.

Lilly was scheduled to be made available for adoption, and she had many adopters asking about her. She would have made anyone a wonderful dog. This is the tough part of fostering: we need to let go of dogs with whom we have developed great relationships in order to make room for the next dog in need of saving. We have been doing this for over 10 years, and it is never easy.

Our first Lab, Ginger, was an abused dog who needed orthopedic surgery. She was treated at OSU and was a wonderful success story. She was an important part of our lives until she died from accidental poisoning. This tragic and devastating event is what got us involved in rescue and motivates us to this day.

Lilly didn't look like Ginger, but she reminded us so much in her spirit and attitude that we couldn't part with her. She now enjoys life as all dogs should, in the comfort of a home with canine companions and people who care. Lilly has a job: she keeps Joey in line and keeps us smiling. Her new nickname is "Wiggles" because that is what she does when you pet her.

Soon we will be bringing in a new foster dog, and Lilly will be responsible for mentoring the new addition to life as it should be for a dog. I am sure she will be up to the task. She has taught us the importance of enjoying life, no matter what.

Ed Nofziger, President, LELRR Inc

If at First You Don't Succeed...

When I first saw Flash a year ago on the Rocky Mountain Lab Rescue website (RMLR), it was like being jolted with lightning. He was *the one*, so I made arrangements to adopt him and subsequently learned more about his past. He had been shuffled around because he nipped a child, though no one saw what really happened. In another home Flash had gone after a dog.

He was sad, terrified, and untrained. A trainer told me Flash would never be able to be with other dogs or go to a dog park. Ouch - I couldn't have that, and I wasn't going to listen. I kept training: classes, the Dog Whisperer, desensitizing. I was open to anything, but his progress seemed minimal. One day Flash went after my delivery man, and then he attacked the guy who bought my motorcycle, biting his arm. I couldn't take the chance of him hurting someone else, so without another solution in sight, I made the painful decision to put him down.

We always walked at night to minimize Flash's interactions with people and dogs. On one of the last walks Flash was to have with me, I ran into my neighbor, Dawn. She said not to put him down just yet and instead suggested we work with her and her well-trained, neutral rescue dog, Yogi. Amazingly Flash was fine with him, and Flash's behavior finally began to change. We introduced more neutral dogs into Flash's life, and Dawn worked with me to change my habits. It was GREAT! I saw hope and was so glad to pass the positive update along to RMLR.

Flash was now ready for a real challenge, so I took him to a dog park and let him watch the dogs play. On the second visit Flash looked calm, so despite my nerves, I let Flash in… and to my relief he played! It was unbelievable and I wished I had my camera. I couldn't believe my eyes. There was not one incident during the entire outing.

The moral of the story is this: try many tactics and don't give up too soon. I am so thankful Dawn and I crossed paths that night, or Flash might not be with me now. He has become the sweetest, goofiest, most loving dog, and now I can even take him to fun events like "Dog Daze of Summer," where he swims in a pool with lots of dogs.

Who would ever have guessed a year ago that Flash would be the perfect companion he is today? At first we didn't succeed, but our trying finally paid off.

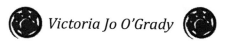 *Victoria Jo O'Grady*

Retriever Recipe: Barley Stew

Christy Cooper, a volunteer with Labrador Retriever Rescue of the Rockies, uses this recipe to keep her dogs happy and healthy, and their tummies full.

Ingredients:

- *1 lb. ground beef*
- *½ - ¾ lb. beef stew meat*
- *1 can pineapple*
- *1 c. barley (uncooked)*
- *Chopped veggies (like zucchini, squash, beets, parsnips, turnips, rutabaga, yucca, carrots, and celery)*
- *2 c. veggie broth*
- *6 eggs, beaten*

Instructions:

Mix the ingredients in a large crock pot. Once it's full, add the veggie broth, and depending on the size, add water almost to the top. Pour the eggs on top of the mixture. Cook on high for 3-4 hours or low for 5-6, stirring occasionally. Put one or two heaping spoonfuls on top of dry dog food in the morning.

Notes:

Lasts for a week in the fridge and can be frozen. Microwave portion to warm it up for a real treat (but watch not to make it too hot). This flavorful recipe is also a great way to hide pills.

Learning Lab

No Shame in Using the Return Policy: Tux was our fifth foster dog. A family adopted him, but then reported back that Tux was hiding in the closet, running away from the kids, and shedding tons of hair. Their vet wanted to put Tux on an anti-anxiety medication, but I knew he just had to come home. Agreeing they weren't the best match, the family promptly returned Tux without guilt or shame. We adopted him and he's been a great big brother to subsequent foster dogs ever since. -*Emi Wyble*

Reward the *Right* Behavior: Bribing a dog to stop an unwanted behavior may actually make matters worse. For example, Butch's original owner would call him to "come" and then offer him treats as a bribe when ignored. By doing this, Butch thought he was receiving a treat for ignoring his owner, so from then on that's what he did – exactly what his owner inadvertently taught him to do. To correct this behavior, I gave the "come" command when Butch was already coming towards me and treated him once he reached me. (You can use a totally new word if you prefer, which often works better.) We practiced on leash - I backed up and called him, knowing I could control the outcome. Once he knew "wait" ("stay" works, too), I had him wait across the room and then called him to come for his meals. Butch is now only rewarded for *completing* the behavior I want and never for doing the opposite. – *Amy Reges*

Learning Lab

Earballs: Charlie was our first blind dog, and we quickly found that he really wasn't disabled at all. The first time he got out of our car was a challenge, but I don't blame him. He had only known us a few hours, and we were asking him to hop into a black abyss. After jumping that hurdle, Charlie fit right into our home. He and our other Lab, Rock, eat together, bark together, and play together like brothers; and Jake, *my* brother, is Charlie's snuggle-buddy and wrestling challenger. The best things for Charlie, though, are toys that make noise – especially a duck that quacks when he squeezes it. If you're considering a blind dog, don't worry. We often forget Charlie is blind. In a way, he "sees" through his ears and other senses.
-Haley Hendershot

Cat-a-What? It's called cataplexy, and it's not a fear of cats. The condition causes Rudy to collapse and fall asleep when he becomes excited. He can see and hear what's going on but can't move his muscles for 2-5 minutes. Sometimes cataplexy sets in at the most inopportune times. For example, six-month-old Rudy once bolted into the street after a cyclist. The excitement caused Rudy's back legs to give out and he fell asleep in the street...at the exact same time a car came around the corner! Though he doesn't have a cat complex, Rudy may just have nine lives – the cyclist jumped off his bike and whisked Rudy out of the road just in the nick of time. *-Tom Puhr*

Learning Lab

Dog Diabetes: We knew there was trouble when Liam started uncharacteristically digging through the trash and opening the refrigerator to steal food. He was eating plenty but looked as though he had lost some weight. The vet diagnosed Liam with diabetes and taught us to control his glucose levels with shots of insulin in the sides of his neck (alternating each time). Liam was so good about it – patiently lying on the floor and eating turkey while we injected him. The insulin allowed him to live out a normal dog life of fun and play. - *Patrick Myers*

Attacking Arthritis: Tux survived Hurricane Katrina, only to be plagued with pervasive arthritis in all of his joints. At the young age of seven, he was in considerable pain. Since we adopted him, his rehabilitation vet has helped him with underwater therapy, land treadmill therapy, pulsed sonar technology, and stem cell therapy. He's is a much happier dog now that his pain is significantly reduced. -*Emi Wyble*

The Gentle Green Giant: Ironically, I picked up Chelsea, a sadly obese, giant, English-type Black Lab, at an eatery. She was being transferred into my care because I committed myself to helping her lose weight before she went on to a forever family. We put Chelsea on regime of daily walks along with the "green bean diet," which consisted of feeding her a can of green beans along with a ½ cup to a cup of dry kibble twice a day. The weight just peeled off, she was never starving, and she quickly regained the figure of a top Amazon supermodel! -*Deb Simpson*

The Breeder Should Have Seen This Coming: Poor Colby is a victim of poor breeding. He's got cataracts, retinal atrophy, and epilepsy, all hereditary conditions that could have been prevented. His epilepsy wasn't too severe and eventually the frequency of his seizures lessened on their own. Unfortunately, the problems with his eyes were not so easy. Our first visit to the ophthalmologist revealed that there was nothing we could do for the cataracts and detached retinas. Then he developed glaucoma and though we lubricated his eyes with drops, the pressure it causes became very painful for Colby. The only solution was to remove his eyes, a procedure that involved removing the eyeballs, putting rubber ball prosthetics into the sockets, and then sewing the lids shut. Recovery was a long haul as he would bump his face on things and whine in pain (even tearing one incision open once), but it was worth it. Eye pain gone, Colby went on to get adopted and live a life full of swimming, hiking, and running on the beach. - *Liz Schwinn*

Not "Just a Dog"

Dedicated to Hutson "Hutty" Kaplan, who was known for his tender disposition and left us far too prematurely on September 26, 2008.

When a dog, especially a rescue dog, comes into our lives, we are afforded a rare chance to make a connection deeper than many human relationships may go.

We are rewarded only when we take time to really listen, to look into his eyes, to watch closely. Moving beyond the thought that he is "just a dog" and arriving at the truth that this living being with emotions and natural instinct has a need for companionship and understanding. Just like us.

They can find friendship anywhere, but they have gifted us with the responsibility of their love and care, along with the key to their hearts and the window to their souls. How truly incredible to make such a strong connection with a species other than our own.

But everything has a balance, and along with this wonderful gift we are also beset by inevitable loss. When they leave, we remain, the sadness immeasurable. Days, weeks of nausea and weakness; tears falling from nowhere. Wishing, hoping for just one more day to see them, smell and touch them, and bury our faces in their fur as we kiss them good-bye. Reminders are everywhere.

They cared even more deeply for us, of course, and trusted us to make every decision about their lives until their final breath. That doesn't make it hurt any less. Knowing this, in the end, is what picks us back up and sends us through the same cycle of love and loss, over and over again. The love being so worth the loss, every time.

Only those who have been through it can truly share your loss and grief, and your eagerness to do it all over again. Those who don't understand were never lucky enough to see what we see; that our pets are much, much more than "just a dog."

 *Peggy Kokernot Kaplan*

"Can we pleeeeez play fetch now?"

About Happy Tails Books™

Happy Tails Books™ was created to help support animal rescue efforts by showcasing the love, happiness, and joy adopted dogs have to offer. With the help of animal rescue groups, stories are submitted by people who have adopted dogs, and then Happy Tails Books™ compiles them into breed-specific books. These books serve not only to entertain, but also to educate readers about dog adoption and the characteristics of each specific type of dog. Happy Tails Books™ donates a significant portion of proceeds back to the rescue groups who help gather stories for the books.

 Happy Tails Books™

To submit a story or learn about other books Happy Tails Books™ publishes, please visit our website at http://happytailsbooks.com.

We're Writing Books about ALL of Your Favorite Dogs!

Schnauzer Chihuahua **Golden Retriever** PUG

DACHSHUND German Shepherd Collie **Boxer**

Labrador Retriever Husky Beagle ALL AMERICAN

Border Collie Pit Bull Terrier Shih Tzu Miniature Pinscher

Chow Chow *Australian Shepherd* Rottweiler Greyhound

Boston Terrier Jack Russell *Poodle* Cocker Spaniel

GREAT DANE Doberman Pinscher Yorkie **SHEEPDOG**

ST. BERNARD Pointer Blue Heeler

Find Them at Happytailsbooks.com!

Make your dog famous!

Do you have a great story about your adopted dog? We are looking for stories, poems, and even your dog's favorite recipes to include on our website and in upcoming books! Please visit the website below for story guidelines and submission instructions! **http://happytailsbooks.com/submit.htm**